THE
CHURCH EXPLORER'S
GUIDE

Arms of St. Oswald

THE CHURCH EXPLORER'S GUIDE

TO SYMBOLS AND THEIR MEANING

FRANK BOTTOMLEY
Illustrated by Connie Green

KAYE & WARD · LONDON

First published in Great Britain by
Kaye & Ward Ltd
21 New Street, London EC2M 4NT
1978

ISBN 0 7182 1182 0 (cased)
ISBN 0 7182 1187 1 (paper)

Set in IBM Press Roman by Reproduction Drawings Ltd, Sutton, Surrey
Printed in Great Britain by Biddles of Guildford

DEDICATED TO THOSE

WHOSE FAITH, HOPE AND LOVE

PRODUCED GOOD WORKS WHICH HAVE

ENRICHED OUR HERITAGE

*All things, as many as pertain to offices and matters
ecclesiastical, be full of divine significations and mysteries, and
overflow with a celestial sweetness; if so be that a man be
diligent in his study of them and know how to draw "honey
from the rock and oil from the hardest stone"*
(W. Durandus, c. 1286).

PREFACE

Thousands of people enjoy visiting old churches. The purpose of this book is to increase their number and their pleasure by enabling them to see rather more and to deepen their understanding of what they see.

Its central theme is not architectural or historical but concerned with meaning — with what the churches and their furnishings are (or were) for and what is their message, particularly through the symbols whose meaning may be lost to alienated modern man. Though many examples are listed, they are deliberately not exhaustive (even were that possible) for there is much pleasure and value in finding things for oneself and drawing one's own conclusions.

Modern society exhibits a growing concern for roots and perhaps cultural roots are more important than genealogical ones. Our ancestors built and worshipped for scores of generations in buildings which have survived in nearly every town and village and as we stand in the quietness of a rural church with its peculiar smell we may well think of our own progenitors who have come before us in anguish and joy, in intercession, thanksgiving and adoration, seeking ideals and strength or confessing weakness and failure. They saw a vision of an ordered and meaningful world in the midst of barbarism, selfishness and pragmatism. We may admire their faith, despise their credulity, vaguely feel part of the past or simply admire the remains of a devoted craftsmanship.

The reasons for our presence may be romantic, aesthetic, historical or even the result of boredom. They might even result from some sort of quest for peace or understanding. It is hoped that this book may make some contribution to all these motives though its particular concern is to arouse empathy so that the explorer may share to some extent in the feelings, belief and message of those who built and adorned these edifices and thus to fill out things which are neglected or omitted in the usual guide-books.

Note

This book is the result of many years spent exploring churches
in all parts of the country. In certain cases it may be that a
church visited twenty years ago and given as an example in this
book has been demolished or its contents removed or changed.
It is almost impossible to ensure against this entirely and if it
should occur the author and publishers make their apology to
their readers in advance. The author would be obliged if
interested readers would communicate to him (via the publishers)
information about errors or notable ommissions.

Archbishop in pontificals

INTRODUCTION

The fuller appreciation of old churches requires both
imagination and knowledge. Neither subjectively nor objectively
does the modern visitor see what their designers intended him to
see. At the height of their development the interiors would
have been full of colour: walls, roof, woodwork and stone
painted and gilded and with harmonious stained glass in all the
windows. The chancel would be almost hidden by a vaulted
screen whose front depicted saints who also gazed from wall
and window. This screen was dominated by a great crucifix with
the attendant figures of St. Mary and St. John beyond which
lay the sanctuary with the High Altar draped in delicate
embroidery and enriched with a reredos of painted and gilded
statuary and itself bearing ornaments of gold and silver. Other
altars, richly furnished, would gleam in the light of tapers and
lamps, brasses would glow with enamels and armorial bearings
would be properly depicted. Services, always with musical
accompaniment, would be almost unceasing and in the intervals
the building would be often busy with secular business. All
this must be remembered as we stand and see the empty niches,
the pale and fragmentary remains of murals and the whitewashed
walls. (Mediaeval churches even had their exteriors painted.)
But more than this mental reconstruction is required to
understand what remains and particularly the range of imagery
which can extend from the Trinity to a man at stool, through
flora, fauna, fabulous beasts and monsters to emblems, signs
and symbols.

It was a mediaeval commonplace that every object perceived
by the senses could be a vehicle conveying thought from the
earthly and transitory to the contemplation of abiding truth.
The mediaeval mind was convinced of the essential integrity of
creation and its emanation from a single divine Source and
believed that all things were bound together in a Great Chain of

Being in which man occupied a nodal point. He was a microcosmic image of the total reality of the macrocosm, his body being made of the same elements as the rest of the material creation and linked with the angelic orders through his spiritual·soul. These convictions, combining existential experience and ratiocination, produced a world of symbols which could be shared by mystics, theologians and illiterate laity. Symbols are open-ended and can convey the verbally prolix or even the ineffable as well as transcending national or written languages. They are thus peculiarly suitable for conveying religious concepts.

Their primary source lay in the Bible and traditional methods of exegesis since they believed that its primary Author was the Holy Spirit who brought it about that the New Testament lay hidden in the Old while the latter was made clear in the New. Thus each fed images into the other, providing Types and Antitypes and from their dialectic truth was manifested. Almost every event and personage in the Old Testament was seen as a prefiguration ('type') of persons and events in the New, especially the redeeming work of Christ. Thus Noah's flood was a type of Baptism, Abraham's would-be sacrifice of Isaac foreshadowed the Father's offering of His only-begotten Son and the Burning Bush could symbolise the Virgin Birth.

The church building itself became a symbol of the entire universe: the roof represented the sky and carried images of the glories of heaven; the nave, devoted to the laity, represented the world and pictured events associated with earthly existence – the life of Christ, the Virgin and other saints. The chancel was seen as heaven, represented in terms of John's apocalyptic vision, and the chancel-arch symbolised death and judgment, the transition from time to eternity, from this world to the next. This division was bridged by the Great Rood, manifesting Christ's Atonement by which man could enter the joys of heaven and reminding him of the price paid by love. Other symbols of time and order were presented, such as the seasons and the stars in their zodiacal courses.

Imagery was also enriched from the formal worship of the Church. The Mass itself was a kind of super-symbol, recalling the moment when Christ instituted a 'memorial' of His redeeming death – uniting present and future in an eternal now. Thus the history of salvation was trans-temporal, not an event in the past but always contemporary. So the soldiers at the Cross or tomb are dressed in contemporary fashion as are the women at the sepulchre. The liturgy, itself dramatic, was extended at the great festivals into quasi-plays where the parts were sung by the sacred ministers. This development, aided by dramatic sermons, developed into the mystery plays whose images and representations provided a source for ecclesiastical sculpture and painting.

If the prime purpose of the church was to provide a location for the sacrifice and sacrament of the altar, its secondary purpose was to teach and motivate — to present the truth and encourage consonant action. Hence faith and works were interlocked in a Christocentric scheme in which symbols were regarded as more effective than words not only because of a prevailing, but overemphasised illiteracy, but because symbols are intrinsically more suitable for the expression of divine truth than limited words.

Besides their advantages, symbols produce problems even when we distinguish between symbol, emblem and attribute. A symbol expressed an abstract idea — the Cross is a symbol of God's love, as is the Pelican. An attribute is a kind of identity disc. Since there is no authentic picture of e.g. St. Hugh of Lincoln he has a swan as an indicator since his pet swan figures in his legend. Thus a figure of a bishop with a swan represents St. Hugh but a swan by itself does not. This kind of substitution is an emblem, as in the case of the Agnus Dei. Unfortunately these usages overlap: often a saint's symbol is the implement of his martyrdom (e.g. St. Lawrence's gridiron or St. Bartholomew's flaying knife) and thus the attribute may become a symbol of martyrdom — of the love that will die for truth. Similarly, the heraldic use of St. Peter's keys or St. Paul's sword can achieve independent existence of an emblematic quality.

The complication is increased by symbols themselves having multiple reference. Thus a lion may point to the Lion of Judah, Christ, and particularly to His incarnation and resurrection. But it may also be an attribute of a recumbent knight, indicating courage, while in other contexts it represents the Devil 'seeking whom he may devour' (I Pet. 5.8). David and Goliath may represent either the antithesis between good and evil or between

work and sloth. Animals and plants often derive their symbolic
meaning from what is said about them in mediaeval bestiaries
and herbals rather than from their natural qualities and even
Scriptural symbolism may be obscure to those ignorant of typology
where Samson carrying off the gates of Gaza symbolises the
Resurrection and the Harrowing of Hell. A particularly frequent
kind of imagery has caused much puzzlement, namely the
grotesque: the grinning faces, the monsters. Such carving on
the exterior of a church may be a kind of prophylactic or
symbolise the church beset by the hosts of Hell but what about
such monstrosities within the sacred edifice? Some are
personified vices, some remind us that evil is not inactive in even
the most sacred situations, some are reminders of the corruption
caused by sin, some may be merely flights of fancy while others
may express deep psychological awareness. In an autobiographical
passage, Thomas Carlyle thus describes the effects of a critical
encounter between faith and the experience that the universe is
alien to man:

> 'I lived in a continual, indefinite, pining fear; tremulous,
> pusillanimous, apprehensive of I know not what; it seemed
> as if all things in the heavens above and in the earth beneath
> would hurt me; as if the heavens and the earth beneath
> were but boundless jaws of a devouring monster wherein I,
> palpitating, waited to be devoured.'

Mediaeval man was much nearer to nature, chaos and sudden
death than any C19 Englishman and though he may not have
been much given to this sort of literary introspection it is
possible that a similar experience may have spawned the horrid
imaginings which still glare down from roof and gable.

It is the chief purpose of this small book to help the
inquisitive find and interpret the wealth of meaning which
survives in the architecture and decoration of churches. We
cannot always give the 'true' interpretation and often 'simple'
subjects which are intrinsically objects of devotion may carry
many overtones e.g. the Last Supper includes the notion of the
continuing Eucharist, Judas' presence is a warning against
sacrilegious communion. Similarly Christ's washing of the
disciples' feet is not merely historical, nor simply an object
lesson in humility but also refers to the cleansing effect of the

sacrament of Penance. Contemporary sermons show that what we might regard as merely a decorative pattern could be a symbol. Some symbols now seem impenetrable and everything is not symbolic — there are 'jeux d'esprit' and plenty of humourous touches as there are plenty of visual puns in heraldry. Conflicting tendencies left their mark too — a sense of topsy-turveydom could be humourous or tragic: there were things to mourn and much to celebrate.

Before appreciating it, it is first necessary to find the symbolism and imagery, and the search should begin some distance from the church before continuing into the churchyard and closely examining the exterior of the church. The south door and its porch always yield something of interest and immediately within the church there may be a stoup. Imagery may be found on font, pulpit and lectern, on capitals, corbels and sepulchral monuments. There may be murals and mediaeval glass or woodwork which merit careful examination and other furniture or decoration, complete or partial, may provoke questions which this handbook answers.

At the end of his perambulation the explorer may be disappointed. Chapels may have been destroyed or converted to alien uses, the fabric might suffer from iconoclasm, neglect or bad restoration. Statues may have been destroyed or mutilated and only fragments of stained glass survive. Painting may have vanished and altar stones be reduced to paving slabs. Shrines have usually been demolished and looted, original vestments and altar furniture confiscated and the original form of the church is sometimes distorted by worldly monuments and pretentious pews. But he is more likely to find evidence of continuing love and care and even wall-paintings which have faded beyond hasty recognition will yield something to those who have patience to wait until the design emerges from the stains and shadows.

Like most good things, church exploration is rewarded by effort and sympathy. The pursuit is unending and full appreciation requires constantly increasing knowledge. Not only must the Bible be known as it was used in the Middle Ages but also some awareness of pagan motifs and folk-tales is required. A little heraldry is useful as is knowledge of Gothic and Lombardic script. Some familiarity with mediaeval literature will not come amiss, including drama, poetry, moral works and sermons. Even these are not the only sources of imagery which was enriched by the visions of mystics, the meditations of saints, the design of miniatures and woodcuts and especially the stories in J. Voreigne's 'Golden Legend'.

Patient investigation will yield a glimpse of the majestic conception that every object in the visible world can be so interpreted as to lead men's thoughts to some heavenly and abiding truth. On a less spiritual level, there is scarcely a church which even now does not remain a treasure-house of uncashable art and craftsmanship, a source of information, interest or admiration. There is no such thing as an 'ordinary' church — every one is unique and has something for the most casual visitor and for those who wish to go beyond appearances each will reveal something of man and perhaps of God.

Arms of St. William of York

SOME PRACTICAL POINTS

These suggestions vary from some having a universal application to others which are for those who are getting caught with the bug of church-exploration.

1. Get a general impression first but look very carefully for details.
2. See if the church has a guide book but don't rely on its accuracy or in the verbal information you might be given though it is always worth hearing.
3. A pair of field glasses is almost essential. Often the most interesting details survive where they were inaccessible to iconoclasts (particularly bosses, corbels, gargoyles and roof details).
4. A camera is useful, particularly if you keep a diary or record of each shot. It is somewhat frustrating to discover, when processed, details you can't locate.
5. A notebook for general purposes will give opportunity for consideration away from the church and making records of your own discoveries.
6. There are certain matters of courtesy. Most churches provide free access and this should not be abused. It is customary to ask for permission for internal photographs and usually required for brass-rubbings. It is good form to ask permission before entering non-public parts of the church (which include sanctuary, vestry and tower). Sometimes fees are required.
7. Naturally, one does not 'explore' while a service is in progress.
8. If the church is locked, the key may be hidden or enquiry in the village will discover its location.
9. If a verger or other person takes you into 'privileged' places or shows you into locked spaces or exhibits hidden treasures such as plate or registers, you should give a tip or make an extra donation to the alms-box.

10. In any case, you will probably wish to help to maintain what has given you pleasure or other benefit.
11. Do not leave without remembering what a church is for whether you share that faith or not:

'We therefore go to church, that we may there ask for pardon of our sins, and assist in the Divine Praises . . . and that we may hear God's decisions on virtues and vices, and learn and receive the knowledge of God, and that we may feed on the Lord's Body' (Durandus).

USING THIS BOOK

Check the plan on page xvi to identify features of the church. The illustrations will also help in the identification if a particular item is not known by name. At the end of the book an index of churches mentioned in the book is provided.

Arms of St. Paul

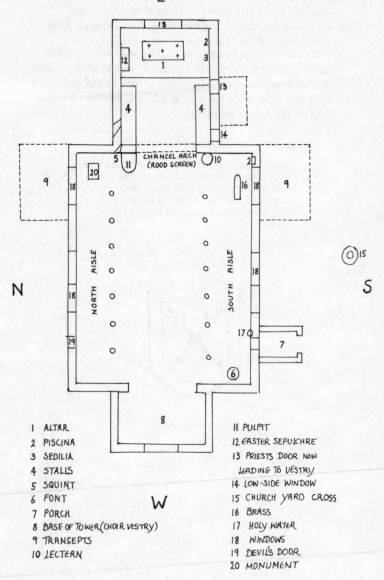

E

18

2
1
3

12

4   4

13

14

5   CHANCEL ARCH   10   2
11   (ROOD SCREEN)

20   16

9   18   18   9

N   18   18   S

19   17

7

6

8

1 ALTAR
2 PISCINA
3 SEDILIA
4 STALLS
5 SQUINT
6 FONT
7 PORCH
8 BASE OF TOWER (CHOIR VESTRY)
9 TRANSEPTS
10 LECTERN

W

11 PULPIT
12 EASTER SEPULCHRE
13 PRIESTS DOOR NOW
   LEADING TO VESTRY
14 LOW-SIDE WINDOW
15 CHURCH YARD CROSS
16 BRASS
17 HOLY WATER
18 WINDOWS
19 DEVIL'S DOOR
20 MONUMENT

15

NORTH AISLE

SOUTH AISLE

ABRAHAM

Patriarch, 'father of the faithful' (Gen. 12-25).
Recipient of God's Covenant (glass: Gt. Malvern,
Worcs.), typified Christ's sacrifice by willingness
to offer his 'only-begotten' Isaac (glass: Gt.
Malvern, Worcs.). Usually represented bearded in
context of Dives & Lazarus (Lk. 16.19-31)
whence 'Abraham's bosom' signifies intermediate
abode of blessed (e.g. Lincoln cathedral (W. front);
Durham cathedral), (choir boss) Alveley,
Salop (frontal); Higham Ferrers, Northants, (brass).

ADAM   see also *Fall*; *Tree, sacred.*

Not only 'first man' but 'all mankind', lord and
steward of created order. Creation of,: Norwich
cathedral (nave boss); St. Neot, Cornw. (glass-
shows Seth placing apple-pips from which wood
of Cross will grow into dead Adam's mouth.) Fall
of : Bledlow, Bucks, (mural); Hook Norton,
Oxon. (font); Leonard Stanley, Glos. (tympanum);
Norwich Cathedral, (nave boss).

AGNUS DEI

Agnus Dei

Lamb with cruciform nimbus, usually carrying
vexillum (q.v.) in front foot. Symbolises Christ as
redemptive sacrifice (Jn. 1.29). Also attribute
of St. John Baptist, name given to wafer stamped
with this emblem, and to musical setting of part
of Mass.
e.g.   bosses: Crondall, Hants.; London .
              St. Andrew Undershaft; Norwich
              St. Peter Mancroft; Selworthy, Som.;
              St. Just-in-Roseland, Cornw.
         bench-end: South Brent, Devon.
         brass: Apsley Guise, Beds., Oxford Merton
              College.
         font: Helpringham, Lincs., Kirkburn,
              Yorks.
         paten: Wyke, Hants.
         tympanum: Ault Hucknall, Derbys;
              Langport, Som.

ALABASTER

Alabaster effigy

Form of gypsum much used in mediaeval England
for statues and carved panels, especially reredoses
(q.v.). There was a notable school of alabaster
carvers at Nottingham. Examples of alabaster
panels and effigies at Ashover, Derbys.; Barmston,
Yorks.; Burton Agnes, Yorks.; Coddenham, Suff.;

Drayton, Berks; Elford, Staffs.; Harewood, Yorks.; Norwood, Staffs.

ALMOND see also *Vesica Piscis.*

Symbol of self-subsistence. An almond-shaped nimbus or mandorla occurs in association with God, especially in Dooms (q.v.). More rarely it surrounds Virgin Mary where it indicates divine approval (Num. 17.1-8). e.g. Prior's door Ely cathedral; Chichester cathedral. An almond encloses a Latin cross at Walton on Wolds, Leics. (font).

ALMS see also *Corporal Works of Mercy; Peter's Pence.*

Practical work of compassion, charitable relief of the poor, money given for this purpose. Poor boxes were provided for the reception of this last e.g. mediaeval: Blythburgh, Suff.; Colston, Notts.; East Kirkby, Lincs.; Hunsdon, Herts.; Selby, Yorks.; Smarden, Kent; Wickmere, Norf.

post-Reformation: Dovercourt, Essex; Halifax, Yorks.; Hargrave, Northants.; Lostwithiel, Cornw.; Pinhoe, Devon; Poynings, Sussex; Sedbergh, Yorks.; Tunworth, Hants.

Alms box

ALMS DISH

Collection plate, offertory dish. Characteristic item of post-Reformation church furniture. (Older meaning of offertory was presentation of bread and wine for use in Mass as symbol of self-oblation). e.g. Canterbury St. Margaret, Kent; Giggleswick, Yorks.; Mortlake, Surrey; Osmaston, Derbys.; Wantage, Berks.

Alms dish

ALPHABET

Signifies the totality of knowledge and truth, or simply absolute totality. It is inscribed in both Latin and Greek in a cross-saltire on the church-floor during its consecration (q.v.). This act is said to refer to Christ's stooping and writing (Jn. 8.6) but is more likely an emphasis on His words: 'I am the Alpha and the Omega, the Beginning and the End' (Rev. 1.8). Occurs on font rims e.g. Rushton All Saints, Northants.; Severnstoke, Worcs. and on church bells e.g. Hennock, Devon; Patrington, Yorks. Its appearance on the interior wall of a church or

chapel may indicate the former use of that area
as a schoolroom.

ALTAR

Mensa

Historically, liturgically and doctrinally, the
altar is not an accessory of the church but
vice-versa, since it symbolises Christ. The first
churches in this country sheltered the altar only;
the congregation stood outside. The placing of
the chief (High) altar decides the orientation (q.v.)
of the church: where the principal altar is, there
is the East end of the church. The altar faces
East because there is the source of light and the
direction of Jerusalem (Ezekiel 43.4) whether
considered as the earthly or heavenly city.

The requirements of 'altar-space' affected the
development of church planning. Transepts
seem to have been invented to accommodate
additional altars which also proliferated in aisles,
before nave pillars, on either side of and above
the rood-screen (q.v.) in and over porches, in
chapels and on table-tombs.

Altar

The upper surface of the altar (mensa =
'table') was usually a single slab of freestone or
marble, symbolising Christ the cornerstone and
the integrity of His church. On it were inscribed
five crosses, symbolising His sacred wounds, and
these were anointed and incensed at the altar's
consecration. Between the central cross and the
front edge was the Altar Sepulchre (q.v.) or
'Confessio' in which relics (q.v.) and
authenticating documents were deposited.
Afterwards the cavity was closed and sealed by a
thin stone slab set flush with the surface.

Because of their objection to what they
called the 'superstitious sacrifice of the Mass' the
Reformers made altars a particular target for
destruction and profanation, replacing them by
'communion tables' (q.v.) and shifting the focus
of the church from altar to pulpit e.g. Congleton,
Cheshire. Yet mediaeval altars survive, some
restored to their original position, at e.g. Arne,
Dorset; Beighton, Derbys.; Callington, Cornw.;
Cookham, Berks.; Corton, Dorset; Cotes-by-Stow,
Lincs.; Dulas, Herefs.; Enstone, Oxon.;
Forthampton, Glos.; Gilstone, Herts.;
Hemingborough, Yorks.; Kimpton, Herts.;
Lackford, Suff.; Longbridge, Wilts.; Maidstone,
Kent; Middleton, Lancs.; Normanby, Yorks.;

Oving, Sussex; Penkevel, Cornw.; Repton, Derbys.; Sall, Norf.; Theddlethorpe, Lincs.; Waterbeach, Cambs.; Whissendine, Rutland; York All Saints.

ALTAR CANOPY (Baldachino, Ciborium, Tester)
In the ancient church the altar was given added dignity, emphasis and respect by being covered with a dome-shaped canopy supported on four pillars. No early ciboria survive in England though the feature has been restored in some modern churches. The middle ages replaced it by a reredos (q.v.), curtains, enrichment of the roof above altar with or without a dependent canopy or tester e.g. Brilley, Herefs.; Clun, Salop.; Ludlow, Salop.; Michaelchurch, Herefs:; Swimbridge, Devon.

The hospital chapel at Sherborne, Dorset has iron bars which probably supported an altar tester.

ALTAR CROSS (Crucifix)
The Cross placed at the centre of the altar symbolises that the eucharistic service which there takes place is a recalling of Christ's immolation on the Cross, the source of our redemption and sanctification, and that Christ is the source and object of Christian devotion. This item of altar furnishing seems almost coeval with Christianity. An apparent crossshrine was found in Pompeii (destroyed 77, AD) and almost every description of early Christian churches gives it special mention.

ALTAR FURNITURE   see also *Vessels, sacred.*
Candles (q.v.) symbolise Christ the Light of the world. Two are said to represent his two natures (human and divine) and the seven, used at pontifical High Mass, the Seven Gifts of the Spirit (q.v.).

Cloths: the surface of the altar is covered with a white linen cloth symbolic of Christ's funeral shroud. Beneath is one of waxed linen (cere cloth) and outside of service-time a third is placed on top as a sort of dust cover (Vesper cloth). The linen cloths also symbolise the church militant which attains proximity to Christ after long processing. A C16 altar cloth survives at Winchcombe, Glos.

Curtains: a symbol of respect for sanctity

Altar cross

(cf. Rood Screen). In the early church the altar was entirely veiled from profane eyes (as it still is in the Orthodox church.) Side curtains (riddells) and occasionally a rear curtain (dossall) have sometimes been restored in imitation of mediaeval usage.

Frontal: as representing Christ the Messianic King and Priest, the altar was sumptuously vested with a frontal in a rich fabric which covered its western face to which was sometimes added a super-frontal which consisted of a narrow strip, often embroidered, which provided a narrower ornament along its top edge. Both these were, and are, decorated with symbols or appropriate inscriptions e.g. Alveley, Salop.; Chipping Camden, Glos.

Lectern or small cushion to support service-book or Missal.

Reredos (q.v.): sculptured panel usually with central crucifix which replaced dossall. Sometimes provided by E. window which descends to level of altar. (see also Alabaster).

Caroline altar rails

ALTAR RAILS   see also *Houselling-cloth*. A low railing separating the Sanctuary (q.v.) from the Quire (q.v.) and a Christian equivalent to the veil separating the Holy of Holies from the Holy Place in the Jewish Temple. The area beyond these rails was restricted to the ministers of the altar and the barrier symbolised the 'separation of things celestial from things terrestrial'. This barrier was rare in the middle ages and the division was indicated, if at all, by a step. The chancel screen with its door or gate was sufficient to prevent profanation by dogs etc. This furnishing proliferated in the Caroline period as a reaction against Puritan irreverence and some of these rails are richly embellished e.g. Astbury, Chesh.; Farnham, Surrey; London St. Stephen Walbrook; St. Decuman's Som.; Woodbury, Devon.

Altar sepulchre

ALTAR SEPULCHRE
Cavity in altar to hold relics (q.v.). The Catacombs had familiarised Christians with the use of a saint's sepulchre as an altar and, when persecution ceased, above the burial places of their dedicatory saints great churches were erected e.g. St. Peter's and St. Paul's in Rome,

St. Cyprian's in N. Africa, St. Martin's in
France, St. Alban's in England. This practice is
the origin of the 'confessio' or crypt (q.v.).
Since all churches, much less individual altars,
could not have the privilege of a whole saint to
themselves, they had to be content with the
small fragments which could be enclosed in the
altar sepulchre. For the antiquity of the idea of
Christ's saints calling from 'beneath the altar',
see Rev. 6.9. The symbolism conveys the idea of
those who were buried with Christ arising with
him through their union in the Mystical Body. e.g.
Altars in the ruins of Jervaulx Abbey, Roche
Abbey, Yorks. Callington, Cornw.; Grantham
(crypt), Lincs.; Madron Well, Cornw.;
Westborough, Lincs.

ANCHORITE   see *Hermit*.

ANGEL

Generic term for purely spiritual beings and also
the name of the lowest order of these beings (see
Angelic Orders). Etymologically, the word means
'messenger' (from God) and they are conceived
as the mediators between the Uncreated God and
the material creation. They are a common symbol
for preachers who convey God's message to
mankind and are also a manifestation of the
unseen world. The mediaeval universe was even
more filled with angels than with demons and
they occur in every part of the church and are
presented in every medium.

Angel

e.g. glass: Chartham, Kent; Odell, Beds.
        brasses: Balsham, Cambs.; Elsing, Norf.;
            Hever, Kent; Little Easton, Essex;
        stone: Beauchamp chapel, Warwick; Percy
            tomb, Beverley, Yorks.; Bradford-on-
            Avon, Wilts
        wood: Knapton, Norf.; Woolpit, Suff.
        embroidery: Cirencester, Glos. (cope).
They occur on bosses, corbels, screens (Hitchin,
Herts.), on murals, stalls (Gresford, Denbighs.;
Beaumaris, Anglesey) and even on a font-cover
(Ewelme, Oxon.). They are appositely located
on many roofs e.g. Disley, Cheshire; Earl
Stonham, Suff.; March, Cambs.; Needham
Market, Suff.; Spalding, Lincs.; St. Decuman's,
Som.; Upwell, Norf.

This proliferation indicates that the mediaeval

consciousness was as filled with the beat of angels' wings as their ears were filled with music. Indeed, there was a connection as angelic musicians are very frequently represented e.g. Buckland Monachorum, Devon; St. Mary Bury St. Edmunds, Suffolk and in the abbeys at Gloucester, Tewksbury and Westminster. Perhaps their most frequently depicted activity is censing – a symbol of pure worship e.g. Chippenham, Cambs.; Sall, Norf.

Carved angels commonly bear heraldic shields, often charged with the Instruments of the Passion (q.v.). Among the objects borne by angels in the roof of All Saints' York are shields, Gospel book, reliquary, chalice, mitre and a variety of musical instruments.

They are frequently represented as partaking in crises in the salvation history of mankind such as the Fall, Incarnation, Redemption, Resurrection, Last Judgment. There appears to be a reliquary of 'angels' feathers' in a glazed recess in one of the nave piers at Pewsey, Wilts.

Angel guardian

ANGEL GUARDIAN
The mediaevals believed that a particular angel was allotted to every human being to strengthen him in temptation, support him in trials and to carry the saved soul to heaven or Abraham's bosom (q.v.) e.g. Ashampton, Beds. (mural); Checkendon, Oxon. (brass); Ely cathedral (tomb); Winchester Cathedral (murals); York St. Michael

ANGELIC ORDERS   see also *Michael, St.*
The notion of nine orders of angels was the result of conflating Coloss. 1.16 and Ephes. 1.21 with elaborations through later writers and commentators particularly the so-called Denys the Areopagite. They were arranged in a hierarchy of three groups of three:

Cherubim, Seraphim, Thrones – closest to God.

Dominions, Virtues, Powers – dominate and govern mankind as a whole.

Principalities, Archangels, Angels – protectors of nations, cities and individuals.

In art they have distinguishing attributes and colours: cherubim are green and usually portrayed as a winged head; seraphim are fiery-red with

7

six wings; thrones are white and carry thrones.

Dominions and Virtues are depicted in glass at Gt. Malvern, Worcs., Seraphim at Clavering, Essex; Southwold, Suff.; Yarnton, Oxon. All nine orders are represented at Barton Turf, Norf. (screen); St. Neot, Cornw.; York St. Michael Spurriergate (glass).

ANGELUS

A thrice-daily (morning, noon, evening) call to prayer in honour of the Incarnation. A bell is rung three times three followed by nine continuous strokes. It is sometimes called the 'Mary' bell (q.v.) and dedicated to the Virgin Mary (q.v.). 'Angelus' is derived from the Latin of the first word of the prayers which begin: 'Angelus nuntiavit Mariam' – 'The angel brought tidings to Mary . . . '

ANGLO-SAXON CROSSES

A loose name given to free-standing crosses which antedate the building of churches, dating from C10 and earlier. Their decorative symbolism is often a curious amalgam of pagan and Christian motifs in which the pagan forms are forced into new meanings so e.g. the wolf and hart become symbols of Christ's passion and the old gods become types of Christ. They often survive in the churchyard or within the church fabric. e.g. Bakewell, Derbys.; Bewcastle, Cumb; Eyam, Derbys.; Gosforth, Cumb.; Guiseley, Yorks.; Halton, Lancs.; Ilkley, Yorks.; Irton, Cumb.; Leeds, Masham, Saxton, Yorks.; Ovingham, Northd.

Some free-standing crosses are Celtic e.g. Lanercost, Cumb.

Anglo saxon cross

ANIMALS   see also *Birds and Beasts; Fabulous Beasts; Monsters.*

Occur in a variety of contexts; as emblems and attributes, as subjects from the Bestiary (q.v.), as commemorations, as characters in popular fables and in genre scenes.

Antelope – his serrated horns could be entangled in bushes as man is enmeshed by his sins e.g. Cawston, Norf. (boss); Ludlow, Salop. (misericord); Manchester cathedral (misericord); Old Cleeve, Som. (boss); Queen Camel, Som. (boss); Walpole St. Peter, Norf. (bench-end);

Widecombe-in-the-Moor, Devon (boss).
Heraldically, badge of Henry VI, candidate for
canonisation (q.v.), e.g. Whimple, Devon;
Wiggenhall St. German, Norf.

Ape (see also Dog-headed man, monkey) —
mirror of unredeemed man, symbolising
bestiality, lust, irrationality, fraud, indecorum.
Often carries satyrical reference and Satan is
sometimes represented as an ape. e.g. Bury
St. Edmund St. Mary, Suff. (boss); Cley, Norf.
(boss); Malmesbury Abbey, Wilts. (tile);
Oxford St. Frideswide (glass); Selby Abbey,
Yorks. (boss).

Bat — cohesive power of common affection e.g.
Chichester cathedral (misericord); Christchurch,
Hants. (misericord); Croscombe, Som. (boss);
Edlesborough, Bucks. (misericord).

Bear — gluttony or sloth e.g. Beverley, Yorks.;
Boston, Lincs.; Bristol cathedral (misericords);
West Lavington, Wilts. (parapet).
Heraldically (with ragged staff), badge of
Warwick. Genre — bear-baiting, bear-dance
e.g. Gloucester cathedral (misericord).

Boar (see also Hog, Pig) courage e.g. Ipswich
St. Nicholas, Suff. (tympanum); Stowlangtoft,
Suff. (bench-end).
Genre in hunting scenes (see Games and
Sports).

Bull — emblem of St. Eustace (Ox, usually
winged, symbol of St. Matthew). Genre in
bull-baiting.

Camel — temperance (St. John the Baptist was
clothed in camel-skin) e.g. Boston, Lincs.
(misericord); Eynesbury, Hunts. (bench-end);
Hereford All Saints (misericord); Isleham,
Cambs. (bench-end); Stowlangtoft, Tostock,
Ufford, Suff. (bench-ends).
    Camel fights unicorn: Manchester
cathedral (misericord) and lions: Lincoln
cathedral, Ripon cathedral (misericords).
    The Magi (q.v.) sometimes ride dromedaries.

Cat — evil lying in wait e.g. Beverley, Yorks.
(misericord); Grappenhall, Cheshire (tower)
— origin of 'Cheshire cat'?

Crocodile — Death, Hell e.g. Kilpeck, Herefs.
(corbels).

Deer (Hart, Stag) — piety, religious aspiration
(Psalm. 42.1) e.g. Beverley, Yorks.
(misericord); Ely cathedral (boss); Melbury

Monkey/ape

Cat and mouse

9

Mediaeval dogs

Bubb, Dorset (cross-shaft).

> With crucifix between horns, attribute of St. Eustace, St. Hubert.
>
> Naturalistic – attribute of St. Julian Hospitaller.
>
> Heraldic – badge of Richard II.

Dog – fidelity, watchfulness e.g. as footrest of female recumbent effigies. Bestiary states that dogs lick their own wounds to heal them e.g. Lakenheath, Suff. (bench-end).

> Attribute of St. Roch and, with flaming torch, symbol of Dominicans (Domini canes = 'hounds of the Lord').
>
> Genre scenes e.g. bosses at Beverley

St. Mary, Yorks.; Broadclyst, Devon; Lacock Abbey, Wilts.; Sherborne, Dorset; Tewkesbury Abbey, Glos.; Walpole St. Peter, Norf.

> As pets, they are sometimes named on tombs and brasses and in this capacity appear e.g. Newcastle-on-Tyne All Saints (brass); Winchester cathedral (boss).

Dog-headed men – probably represent baboons and symbolism similar to that of monkeys (q.v.) The question whether baboons had souls was debated in the Middle Ages. Another theory is that they represent travellers' tales of Icelanders dressed in their customary 'parkas'. e.g. Bristol cathedral (boss).

Elephant – symbol of Christ, can also symbolise Adam, mankind redeemed by Christ, chastity. e.g. Dunkeswell, Devon (font); Gosberton, Lincs. (gargoyle); South Lopham, Suffolk (Poppy Head); Ottery St. Mary, Devon (pier carving). Elephant and castle refers to war animals of Indians and Persians. 'Rook' (castle) in chess is derived from Persian word for elephant. e.g. Beverley, Yorks; Exeter cathedral; Gloucester cathedral; Holme Hale, Norf. Manchester cathedral (misericords); Ripon cathedral (stall); Tong, Salop. (brass).

Fox – cunning and guile, Devil e.g. Alne, Yorks (door); Beverley St. Mary, Yorks (boss); Cley-next-the-sea, Norf. (boss); Whalley, Lancs. (misericord). Reynard the Fox e.g. Bristol cathedral; Carlisle cathedral; Windsor St. George, Berks.; (misericords). A preaching fox often represents satire against Mendicant Orders e.g. Brent Knoll, Som.; (bench-end).

Fox

Frog – heresy, corruption e.g. Edlesborough,
Bucks (misericord); Norwich cathedral
cloisters (boss). Represented as consuming
corpses on sepulchral monuments and
apparently in connection with necromantic
medicine e.g. Windsor St. George, Berks
(misericord).

Goat – Christian browsing on bush of truth
e.g. Windsor St. George, Berks. (misericord).

Hare (Rabbit) – lust. 'Natural' hares appear at
Pennant, Montgom. in church of St. Melangell
who was a protectress of hares.

Hart – see Deer.

Hare

Hedgehog – Bestiary said it fed young on grapes
impaled on prickles – illustrated Oxford
New College (misericord).

Hippopotamus – creature of two elements (man?)
e.g. Windsor St. George (misericord)

Horse – can symbolise lechery (see Centaur s.v.
Fabulous Beasts)

Horse

Hyena – symbol of manifold evil: hypocrisy,
impurity, inconstancy, wantonness, avarice.
An eater of corpses e.g. Alne, Yorks.
(sculpture); Carlisle cathedral (misericord);
Queen Camel, Som. (boss).

Ibex – protected by its horns when it falls over
precipices; symbol of learned men cushioned
by two Testaments e.g. Kings Lynn,
St. Nicholas, Norf. (bench-end).

Lamb – see Agnus Dei

Leopard – symbol of evil; sin, cruelty, Antichrist
e.g. Dartmouth, Devon (door ironwork);
N. Cerney, Glos. (buttress).

Lion – perhaps most frequently occurring animal
in imagery. Symbol of Christ ('Lion of Judah')
and specifically of His resurrection since it was
believed to bring dead cubs to life three days
after death by breathing on them e.g. Ampney
St. Mary, Glos. (tympanum). May also
symbolise Devil (I Pet. 5.8) e.g. Sutton-by-Caistor,
Northants. Winged lion is emblem of St. Mark
while a natural one is attribute of St. Jerome.
Common heraldic device and as foot supporter
on recumbent effigies it symbolises courage.
Many mediaeval lions closely resemble dogs since
few sculptors had seen them and dogs, suitably
'made up', stood in for lions in mediaeval drama.
e.g. Oxford Christchurch (boss); Durham
cathedral (knocker); Eardisley, Herefs. (font);

Lion

11

Manchester cathedral, Windsor St. George, Berks. (misericords).

Lion fighting man probably illustrates Samson (type of Christ) story (Judges 14.5ff.) e.g. misericords: Exeter, Lichfield, Norwich cathedrals. In conflict with dragon symbolises struggle between good and evil e.g. Beverley Minster, Yorks. (corbel); Carlisle, Lincoln cathedrals (misericords). Said to eat monkey when sick: Windsor St. George, Berks. (misericord).

Monkey (see also Ape) — usually satirical reference and occurs in attacks on physicians. A monkey's funeral is portrayed in North aisle glass York Minster which also shows monkey holding owl (lust producing spiritual blindness?). Other examples: Beverley St. Mary, Yorks.; Manchester cathedral, (misericords); Stowmarket, Suff. (stall).

Panther — enemy of dragon and said to hide three days and then attract all animals by its scent. Symbol of Christ in tomb, resurrection, and calling mankind e.g. Alne, Yorks (door); Newton, Yorks. (sculpture); Tewkesbury, Glos. (boss).

Pard — panther-lioness hybrid, distinguished by its branching tail. Like all hybrids an evil symbol: in this case, blood-lust.

Pig

Pig (see also Hog) — often boar, sow and farrow who, in West country, marked divinely chosen church-site and, in commemoration, they are portrayed on bosses and bench-ends e.g. Broad Clyst, Sampford Courtney, Spreyton, Ugborough, Devon. Pig at Winwick, Lancs. (tower) is supposed to have helped transport building materials.

It also occurs in genre scenes: Exeter cathedral (boss); Ripon cathedral (misericord); Selby, Yorks. (boss); Wootton Courtney, Som. (boss).

Playing musical instruments (satirical?) as in Pig and Whistle e.g. Beverley St. Mary, Yorks. (boss).

Rabbit (see also Hare) — may symbolise lust or soul in danger. Also occurs in genre scenes of hunting. e.g. Combs, Suff. (bench end).

Ram

Ram — symbol of Christ: sometimes Agnus Dei (q.v.) is metamorphosed into ram with reference to sacrifice of Isaac (Gen. 21.13).

Serpent

The Annunciation

Rat (Mouse) – usually symbolises destructiveness of evil gnawing away substance. Emblem of modern woodcarver (Thompson of Kilburn, Yorks). Boss at Meavy, Devon has grotesque head with large ears from which the head and tail of a mouse emerge (='empty head'?).

Scorpion – evil and treachery.

Serpent (snake) – aboriginal symbol of evil but serpent of Eden is always shown as Dragon (q.v. under Fabulous Beasts) and because serpent was said to slough off old skin by scraping through narrow crack in rocks it could symbolise regeneration, putting off sin e.g. Ashover, Derbys. (font).

Sheep – symbolise Christians in early art but appear only incidentally in mediaeval imagery, apart from Agnus Dei (q.v.) e.g. Nativity scenes, occasional genre scenes and on brasses of prosperous wool-merchants e.g. Northleach, Glos.

Squirrel – prudence, but may be simply genre scene e.g. Exeter cathedral, Lacock Abbey, Wilts.; Oxford Christchurch, Latin chapel, (bosses).

Tiger (tigress) – believed to be susceptible to deceit by its own reflection and therefore symbolises man taken in by unreal ('vanities') e.g. Lakenheath, Suff. (bench-end); Queen Camel, Som. (boss); Wendens Ambo, Essex; Wiggenhall St. Germans, Norf. (bench-ends).

Wolf – said to bite own paws to make them tread more softly, symbolises rapacity, Satan e.g. Faversham, Kent (misericord). When guarding head, associated with St. Edmund e.g. Walpole St. Peter, Norf. (bench-end).

Assorted natural animals (rats, mice, weasels, woodlice) occur at Hereford All Saints (misericords) and there are remains of unidentifiable symbolic animals at Eastry, Kent (mural). See also Virtues and Vices. Animals may form part of a rebus (q.v.).

ANNUNCIATION   see also *Lily, Rosary, Virgin Mary*

The announcement by the archangel Gabriel informing Mary that she is to be the Mother of God's Son (Lk. 1.26ff.). Represents the beginning of the New Creation and symbolises human co-operation in that work. Christ's conception was believed to take place as Mary said 'Behold the handmaid of the Lord. Be it unto me according to Thy Word' (Luke 1.38). Hence this instant was considered as the most important moment in salvation history. The lily-pot in the imagery seems to have been an English introduction. e.g. Adlingfleet, Yorks. (porch); Ashampstead, Berks; Dale, Derbys. (murals); Finendon, Northants. (font); Hovingham, Yorks. (sculpt.); Norwich St. Peter Mancroft (glass); Ross-on-Wye, Herefs. (tomb-chest); Southwell, Notts. (capital); Upavon, Wilts. (font); Wiston, Suff. (mural). Also appears on panels of rood-screen (e.g. Bradninch, Devon).

ANTETYPE   see *Scripture, Type.*

ANTISEMITISM
Arose from the Jews' involvement in the death of Christ and their alleged corporate acceptance of responsibility for this act (Matt. 27.25). Constantly reminded of this and forgetful that Christ's mother and the first Christians were Jews, the mediaeval world maintained its prejudice by stories of continuing Jewish blasphemy, sacrilege and blood sacrifices of Christian children e.g. legends of St. Hugh of Lincoln and St. William of Norwich (represented Loddon, Norf. on rood-screen). Jewish sacrilege against Blessed Sacrament on mural at Friskney, Lincs.

APOCALYPSE
The Revelation of St. John – the last book of the Bible – whose imagery is a much used source for graphic representation. Ch 4, v7, is the source of the Evangelistic symbols (q.v.) and the Apocalypse also provided the conflict between Michael and the Dragon (12.7ff.) which can symbolise either the struggle between the spiritual powers of Heaven and Hell or the persecution of the church on earth. Further images from this book include the twenty-four elders who symbolise the Doctors (q.v.) of the Old and New Testament, the white robes of the redeemed, the seven lamps before the throne which were taken to symbolise the seven gifts of the Holy Spirit (q.v.), the sea of glass which indicated baptism. The book may derive its

The Apocalypse:
seven lamps before
the throne

images from the liturgical practice of the early church: presbyters about the throne (altar), choir singing alleluia, saints crying from beneath the altar etc. and we thus have an interesting example of practice affecting symbolism which, in turn, affected practice, as well as of the interaction of prayer and belief. e.g. Copford, Essex (mural); Egleton, Rutland (tympanum); Kempley, Glos. (mural) and the rich selection of roof-bosses in the cloisters of Norwich cathedral.

Other apocalyptic images are 'the woman clothed with the sun' and the Lamb 'as it had been slain'. (see Virgin Mary, Agnus Dei).

APOSTLES, SAINTS, PROPHETS   see also
Apostles, twelve; Creed; Saints; Prophets.
In general, these characters typify witness to the Truth and they are depicted in every possible material and location: arches, niches, fonts, rood-screens, murals, tombs, vestments (e.g. Astley, Warks. (stalls); Sutton Benger, Wilts. (vestments). It was a common practice to alternate prophets and apostles, especially in Creed series.

APOSTLES, TWELVE
Symbolise foundations of church in orthodoxy and truth and historical continuance from Christ. They are identified by attributes which are often the traditional instruments of their martyrdom. (e.g. Beeston Regis, Norf.)

Peter,

James,

John,

Andrew,

Peter: keys (Matt. 16.18tf.); cock (Matt. 16.34.74ff.); inverted cross (Jn. 21.18ff.) chief of the apostles, Christ's steward, rock on which church is built. e.g. Bere Regis, Dorset (roof).

James (the Great): pilgrim's cloak and hat, scallop-shell (badge of his popular shrine at Compostella, Spain) Patron of pilgrims. e.g. Plymtree, Devon (screen); Syde, Glos. (glass).

John: cup with emergent dragon (legend of failure to poison him); chalice without dragon refers to his eucharistic teaching (Jn. 6)). A cauldron refers to failed attempt to martyr him in boiling oil. As evangelist, eagle emblem. e.g. East Brent, Som. (glass); Tong, Salop. (tomb); York All Saints' (glass). Also appears with Virgin Mary at foot of Cross (see Rood).

Andrew: cross saltire on which he was crucified, holding fish in reference to calling. Patron of missionaries. e.g. Greystoke, Cumb. (glass);

Apostles, Saints, Prophets

Matthew,

Thomas,

Phillip,

James,

Simon

Matthias

Matthias

Ranworth, Norf. (screen).

Matthew: spear or axe from his legendary martyrdom, holding money-bag in reference to calling as publican (tax-collector). As evangelist, his emblem is a man or angel. e.g. Greystoke, Cumb.; Norwich, church museum (glass); Westminster Abbey (statue – with spectacles!).

Thomas: spear or arrow from his legendary martyrdom in India where he went as missionary; book in reference to evangelistic activity; tools of carpenter or builder – similar symbolic reference. Patron of carpenters and builders. e.g. Exeter cathedral, west front (statue); Ranworth, Norf. (screen).

Phillip: loaves and/or fishes (Jn. 6.5-9) e.g. Ranworth, Norf.; staff and book (missionary activity) e.g. Cawston, Norf. (screen). Tau-cross on which, traditionally, he was crucified e.g. Blythburgh, Suff. (stalls).

James (the Less); fuller's club with which he was beaten to death e.g. Ranworth, Norf. (screen).

Bartholomew: butcher's flaying knife with which he was flayed alive, sometimes represented carrying skin on arm. e.g. Beeston Regis, Norf. (screen).

Simon (Zelotes): saw with which he was bisected, book representing missionary activity, fish or oar referring to calling. e.g. Ranworth, Norf. (screen).

Jude (Thaddeus): club by which he was martyred, boat referring to calling and/or missionary travels, cross on end of long staff. e.g. York Minster choir. (glass).

Matthias (replacement for Judas): axe or sword referring to decapitation. e.g. Blythburgh, Suff. (stalls).

Apostles also occur at Carleton Rode, Norf. (screen); Elsing, Norf. (font-cover); Malmesbury, Wilts. (tympanum); Malvern, Worcs. (glass); Plympton, Devon (screen); King's Lynn, Norf. (brass); Long Sutton, Som. (pulpit); Rendcomb, Glos. (font); Strensham, Worcs. (screen); and all twelve were represented on murals at Beddington, Surrey; Birchington, Kent; Covenham St. Bartholomew, Lincs. (font); Hadleigh, Essex; Kimpton, Herts.; Nether Wallop, Hants.; Pershore, Worcs. (font); Peterborough Cathedral (Hedda stone); Southease, Sussex.

ARCHITECTURE

Dating may be helped if the following, very rough, approximations of the dates of the various styles of mediaeval architecture are kept in mind:

Saxon up to 1066

Norman (Romanesque) from about 1066 to about 1190 with a transitional period from about 1145 to 1190 leading to

Early English (Pointed) from about 1190 to 1280, followed by

Decorated from about 1280 to 1380 and *Perpendicular* from about 1380 to about 1550.

Styles changed slowly and some parts of the country lagged behind in the acceptance of new fashions.

Architectural features are represented on bosses at Bristol St. Mary Redcliffe; Congresbury, Som.; Sherborne Minster, Dorset.

Gothic architecture is essentially geometric in design. God was considered as the eternal geometer and was sometimes represented with the tools of the architect: compasses, plumb-line and set square. Architectural features are often symbolic (see Church Symbolism, Door etc.).

Architecture: windows

ARK   see also *Ship*

The Ark

Noah's Ark is a type of the Church (1 Peter 3.20) e.g. Norwich cathedral nave (boss); York St. Michael Spurriergate (glass).

ARMA VIRGINIS

The age of chivalry wished to ascribe armorial bearings to the Queen of Heaven and Queen of Love and therefore attributed emblematic heraldry to the Virgin Mary. It usually took the form of a heart, often winged and pierced with a sword (Lk. 2.35). Much of this sacred heraldry was destroyed by reforming iconoclasm but it occasionally survives in unattainable bosses e.g. Beverley St. Mary, Yorks.; Bristol and Hereford cathedrals.

ASCENSION OF CHRIST   see also *Creed*

Represents the taking of full human nature (not merely the soul) into heaven as a consequence of Christ's Death and Resurrection. e.g. Launcells, Corn. (bench-end); Lincoln

17

Ascension

Assumption: boss

cathedral (misericord); Norwich St. Helen (boss); Pinvin, Worcs. (mural).

ASHES
Their application is a symbol of mourning and repentance for sin taken over from Jewish practice. On Ash Wednesday, the first day of Lent (q.v.), Mass is preceded by the Ceremony of the Ashes in which the foreheads of those present are marked with ashes in the shape of a small cross, indicating the penitential nature of this liturgical season. The ashes are made from the palms of the previous Palm Sunday (q.v.) reminding us of the swift transmission in earthly life from joy to sorrow. They constitute a sacramental (q.v.) and are administered with the words: "Remember man that dust thou art and unto dust shalt return". They thus symbolise bodily death and the brevity of human life compared with eternity.

ASSUMPTION
It is an extremely ancient belief that the body of the Virgin Mary did not rest in a grave but was assumed into heaven because of her freedom from sin which 'brought death into the world'. According to legend, doubting Thomas did not believe this either and was only convinced when he received her girdle from heaven. Devotion to the Assumption was extremely popular in mediaeval England and the festival was nationally celebrated long before it was kept by the whole Western Church on August 15th. Its observance increased with the development of courtly (romantic) love and devotion to the Virgin seems to have advanced pari passu with this phenomenon. After C12 Mary was hailed as Star of the Sea, Moon among the stars of heaven, Sun among the seven planets chief. A sermon of the following century says:

'The departure of this maid was measured without dissolution, her eyes declaring total chastity, her face full of delights and amiable to angels. The words which she spoke were most sweet and easy, ever sounding to the thanking of God. No man should have woman in despite; for it is no wisdom to despise that which God loveth.' The belief is obviously associated with symbols of motherhood, the exaltation of the feminine principle and the celebration of the entry of the first simple human being into highest heaven. It was an extremely common subject of graphic art but because of reforming Mariophobia its expression now survives mainly in bosses e.g. North Moreton, Berks; Peterborough cathedral (porch); York Minster (pulpitum) but there are other examples: Brook, Kent; Curdworth, Warks. (murals); East Harling, Norf. (glass); Sandford, Oxon (sculpture); Stanford, Northants. (glass); Tiverton, Devon.

The assumption was associated in popular piety with the Coronation of the Virgin (see Rosary) which was imaged in murals at e.g. Black Bourton, Oxon.; Brook, Kent.

ATONEMENT   see also *Cross, Rood.*
It is the heart of Christian belief that 'God was in Christ reconciling the world unto Himself' and the central symbol of this belief is the Cross on which God incarnate died as a perfect and sufficient sacrifice to remove man's alienation. Consequently, the Cross is the Christian symbol 'par excellence', but other common symbols refer to the Atonement such as the Crown of Thorns, the Instruments of the Passion (q.v.) and the Five Wounds (q.v.).

AUMBRY
Also called hutch, locker, ministerium. Used of free-standing presses (e.g. Wensley, Yorks.) but principally refers to cupboards in the thickness of the chancel wall. Such cupboards, especially if they were located in the north wall, were used for the safe-keeping of altar vessels. Aumbries were also sometimes used for the reservation of the Blessed Sacrament (q.v. and cf. Pyx) and for the protection of relics (often in East wall). Similar cupboards in the vicinity of the font were for the accessories of baptism: oil, salt, etc. Long narrow cupboards at the West end of the church were lockers for banner-staves. Aumbries are very frequent in the south wall of the chancel e.g. Aston, Norf.; Flore, Northants.; Little Bytham, Lincs.; Richmond, Yorks.; Stanford-in-the-Vale, Berks.; Thanet Minster, Kent; Trunch, Norf. Bibury, Glos. deserves mention for its possession of eight aumbries in the chancel.

Aumbry

AUREOLE   see *Halo*.

'Ave Maria
Gratia'

AVE

Refers to Gabriel's greeting to Mary and most commonly to the most popular Marian prayer composed from the conjunction of Lk. 1.28 and 42 with the addition of a brief intercession. The recitation of the 'Hail Mary' was even used for timing accurate cooking and the greatest theologians commented on its spiritual significance and value. Mediaevals soon latched on to the symbolic possibilities of the fact that Ave is Eva (Eve) reversed: that Mary's obedience to the will of God cancelled out Eve's disobedience; that Mary was the Second Eve ('Mother of all living') as Christ was the second Adam, etc.

The Rosary (q.v.) consists chiefly in reciting 'Aves' in groups of ten, interspersed with the Lord's Prayer and the Gloria (Decade). The 'Ave bell' was the Angelus (q.v.).

BANNER

Consecrated banners date from time of first Christian emperor, Constantine, who seems to have attributed his decisive victory to their aid (325 AD). As with the Israelite ark, such objects were considered numinous and in the Dark Middle Ages they were believed to aid the army bearing them. At other times they were kept above an altar or saint's tomb and their staves stored in lockers (see Aumbries). Modern ecclesiastical banners are usually kept near an altar and in Anglican churches tend to be restricted to the Mothers' Union. Regimental colours preserved or 'laid up' in churches, often high in the roof, are a hangover of the mediaeval tradition.

Banner

BAPTISM   see also *Font, Sacraments*.

The sacrament of admission into the Christian church, 'Christening' or incorporation into the Body of Christ. Symbolism of washing and of emerging from death into life. Its importance was emphasised by linking its occasion with the ceremonies of the Easter Vigil (Holy Saturday) and subsequently of Whitsunday (Pentecost). The adult candidate was prepared by a period of training and instruction (catechumenate). The instruction (catechesis) was probably linked with the Liturgical Year (q.v.) and concluded by an examination and the rectitation of the Apostles' Creed (q.v.). Originally, the rite was confined to Easter Eve and Whitsun Eve, apart from emergencies, but increasing numbers led to its extension to the Sunday after Easter (Dominica in albis – 'Sunday of the White Robes' cf. Whit(e)sunday) and finally, with infant baptism becoming the norm, to any Sunday. The candidate was presented by sponsors or god-parents who gave him a new *Christian* name as a symbol of his rebirth and he was clothed in a white robe (chrysom) of which the Christening gown is a relic. The elaborate ceremony involved the use of salt and water and in cities a special building (baptistery) was sometimes provided for its setting. No separate baptisteries survive in England though the chapels over Holy Wells (q.v.) may once have served this purpose. The font (q.v.) containing the baptismal water is always placed by the main church door to symbolise that baptism effects entry into the Church.

Beak head

BEAK HEAD

Characteristic Norman (Romanesque) ornament, especially on arches (e.g. Adel, Yorks.; Asthall, Oxon.; Healaugh, Yorks.; Kilpeck, Herefs.; Tickencote, Rutland.; Windrush, Glos.). Its significance is obscure except that it seems to be a continuation of a pagan motif. Some of these heads have been related to a winged, beaked horse-god of the Celtic period which appears on a Romano-British roundel found at Santon Downham, Suff.

BEASTS   see also *Animals, Bestiary, Dragons, Fabulous Beasts.*

A frequent decorative feature along with birds (e.g. Barfreston, Kent). They may be purely decorative or represent a 'jeu d'esprit' of the craftsman. When symbolical they indicate the wondrous variety and exuberant joy of creation. In another function, birds may symbolise the things of heaven: the spiritual and supernatural, while beasts refer to the fleshly and natural things of earth.

Ape

BELL

In the Middle Ages, church bells were very solemnly dedicated: blessed, anointed and given names of saints. They were believed to have a sacramental (q.v.) significance and possess quasi-supernatural powers:

'The reason for consecrating and ringing bells is this: that by their sound the faithful may be mutually cheered on towards their reward; that the devotion of faith may be increased in them; that their fruits of the field and their minds and bodies might be defended; that the hostile legions and all the snares of the Enemy might be repulsed; that the rattling hail, the whirlwinds, and the violence of the tempests and lightning might be restrained; the deadly thunder and blasts of wind held off; the Spirits of the storm and the Powers of the Air be overthrown; and such as hear them may flee for refuge to the bosom of our Holy Mother the Church, bending every knee before the standard of the Holy Rood.' (Durandus).

They were also used to provide warning and alarm (tocsin), for the curfew (usually 9 p.m.) which also signalled 'time' in ale-houses, as well as for devotional and celebratory purposes. By coding and using different bells they could indicate christenings, marriages, deaths and funerals, festivals and specific 'hours'. There were peals for summoning council, call to market, to gleaning or to indicate that the town oven was hot. They called people to commemorate the Incarnation (Angelus q.v.), to pray for a passing soul, or to make their confessions before Lent. The custom of change-ringing is peculiar to England, but some mediaeval peals played hymn tunes.

Bells often bear religious imagery as well as trade-marks of bell-founders and names and prayers. They were usually housed in a tower built for this purpose which might be detached from the church (e.g. West Walton, Norf.) but could be hung from a simple bell-cote (e.g. Kelmscott, Oxon.) or in a bell-cage (e.g. Brympton D'Evercy, Som.).

They are a symbol of Christian preachers and of the power of truth and their inscriptions proclaim faith and ask for saintly intercession (e.g. Theddlethorpe, Lincs.; Shapwick, Dorset).

Bell

Bell decoration

A bell-ringer appears at Belton, Lincs (font); Winwick, Lancs. (Saxon cross); and there is a bell-founders' window in north aisle of York minster.

Bell, sacring

BELL, SACRING   see also *Lychnoscope*.
External church bell rung during Mass so that 'at the Elevation of the Body of Christ the people who have not leisure daily to be present at Mass may, wherever they are in houses or fields, bow their knees' (Peckham, 1281). A sacring bell is sculptured on the font at Cley, Norf. There is no uniform location of this particular bell but its most common position was in a bell-cote at the junction of nave and chancel roofs (e.g. Preston, Glos.; Idbury, Oxon.). It could be placed in choir wall (Tewkesbury Abbey, Glos.), transept wall (Milton Abbas, Dorset), over porch (Northleach, Glos.), in nave interior with exterior louvred opening (Findon, Sussex) or with the others in the belfry with a door or squint looking into the church (Shere, Surrey).

BELL, SANCTUS
Handbell or small hanging bell to indicate to congregation stage of Mass which had been reached. (Mass in Latin and some parts inaudible). e.g. Hawstead, Suff.; Salhouse, Norf. (choir screen); Bottesford, Lincs; cf. Portishead. Som.; Scarning, Norf.

Bench end with foxes

BENCH ENDS   see also *Poppy Heads*.
The vertical surfaces formed by the ends of mediaeval seating (in which Somerset is particularly rich) provided an area for architectural, naturalistic and symbolic design well worthy of special study. e.g. Abbotsham, Devon.; Ashmanhaugh, Norf.; Bishops Lydeard, Broomfield, Som.; Blythburgh, Suff.; Braunton, Devon.; Crowcombe, Som.; Croxton Kerrial, Leics.; Davidstow, Cornw.; Granby, Notts.; Hardley, Norf.; Hemingborough, Yorks.; Horning, Norf.; Laneast, Cornw.; Milverton, Som.; Padstow, Cornw.; Osbournby, Lincs.; St. Breward, St. Legan, St. Teach, Cornw.; Sutcombe, Devon.; Water Newton, Bucks.; Wimbotsham, Norf.; Winthorpe, Lincs.; Zennor, Cornw.

Bestiary

BESTIARIES

Mediaeval Books of Beasts whose contents
were collected for their wondrous or moral
qualities rather than for zoological accuracy.
They seem to have originated in a C5 work from
Alexandria called the 'Physiologus' which was
used, copied and added to throughout the
Middle Ages and into early modern times. Its
value for didactic purposes far outweighed its
manifest inaccuracies and legendary quality. It
is the origin of the popular and widespread
series of fabulous beasts (q.v.) whose symbolism
depends almost entirely on knowledge of the
accepted ideas enshrined in the bestiaries. e.g.
bosses at Cawston, Norf.; Old Cleeve, Som.;
Queen Camel, Som.; Sampford Brett, Som.;
Widdecombe-in-the-Moor, Devon; Wootton
Courtney, Som.

BIBLE OF THE POOR

A title sometimes given to the richly sculptured
west front of Wells cathedral which survives as a
classic example of the didactic art and
systematic symbolism which one prodigally
enriched the smallest churches and chapels. The
foundation of this particular graphic praise of the
Redeemer is a tier of Old Testament. Prophets
who foretold the coming of Christ. In other
niches stand the martyrs, witnesses to the power
of His redemptive work, together with saints and
confessors who include kings and queens, nobles
and ecclesiastics. The spandrels of the arcades
are occupied by representations of the angelic
hosts and typical scenes from the Scriptures.
The upper part of the facade represents the
Second Coming of Christ and shows the general
resurrection, the nine orders of angels in Heaven,
the apostles and — to crown and unite the whole
composition — Christ the King and Supreme
Judge.

BI-CORPORATES   see also *Heads.*

A grotesque monster in which a single head
serves two bodies. This invention seems more
decorative than symbolic (though grotesques
and composites normally symbolise evil) and
arises from the exigencies of design. It is
frequent on roof-bosses and appears elsewhere
e.g. capitals (Barfreston, Kent).

Crane

Dove

Eagle

BIRDS   see also *Beasts*.

Often naturalistic e.g. Bicknoller, Som. (boss); Chester cathedral (misericord); Exeter cathedral ambulatory (boss); but they may be heraldic, including rebuses (q.v.), e.g. Amesbury, Wilts.; Beverley, Yorks. and West Country (bosses) and are frequently symbolic:

Blackbird — temptation.

Cock — watchfulness, associated with St. Peter and Passion of Christ (cf. I Pet. 4.7). May be heraldic — Noseley, Leics. (bench-ends).

Crane — vigilance. Sentinel crane was believed to hold stone in claw which dropped if it drowsed e.g. Denston, Suff.; Lincoln cathedral; (misericords).

Dove — Christian soul. When haloed, the Holy Spirit. Drinking from chalice or pecking grapes: Holy Communion e.g. Bishopstone, Sussex (grave-slab); Kirkburn, Yorks. (font).

Eagle — Christian soul rising in contemplation, symbol of John the Evangelist. Was believed to renew its youth by ascending towards sun until old plumage and eye-cataract was burnt away when it then plummetted into a fountain e.g. Alne, Yorks. (door); Higham Ferrers, Northants. (misericord); Forrabury, Cornw. (altar). Manchester cathedral (stall-end) refers to legend of baby found in eyrie.

Egg — resurrection and new life, hence Easter and Pace (Pasch) eggs.

Goose - vigilance. Attribute of St. Martin of Tours.

Hawk — evil or the Devil stooping on the unwary, or naturalistic. Represented with rabbit or other small animal in its talons.

Hen and chickens — Christ's love for His people (Matt. 23.37) e.g. Beverley, Yorks.

Hoopoe — filial piety e.g. Carlisle cathedral; Windsor St. George, Berks. (misericords).

Ibis — man who will not abandon sins e.g. Lavenham, Suff.; Windsor St. George, Berks.; (misericords).

Ostrich — disregard of earthly things e.g. Stratford, Warks.; Westminster Henry VII chapel; Windsor St. George, Berks. (misericords).

Owl — Satan and devils who prey on souls, spiritual blindness e.g. Bury St. Edmunds St. Mary, Suff.; Cley-next-the-sea, Norf. (bosses);

Edlesborough, Bucks.; Hemington, Northants. (misericords); Lacock Abbey, Wilts. (boss).

Peacock — immortality. Belief that its flesh was incorruptible. e.g. Cartmel, Lancs. (misericord); Chester cathedral (font).

Pelican — Christ, Divine self-sacrificial love. Believed to feed young with its own blood, hence may symbolise Eucharist. Also heraldic (arms of Bp. Fox) Winchester (bosses). e.g. Aldington, Kent (pulpit); Lincoln cathedral (misericord); Norwich cathedral (lectern); Ufford, Suffolk (font-cover); Warbleton, Sussex (brass); York All Saints' (misericord).

Pelican in its piety

Popinjay (paraqueet) — reverence, e.g. Wells cathedral (misericord).

Swan — no clear symbolic significance. Attribute of St. Hugh of Lincoln, heraldic or reference to romance of Swan Knight e.g. Bury St. Edmunds St. Mary, Suff. (boss); Burwell, Cambs. (boss); Exeter cathedral (misericord); Lacock Abbey, Lacock Church, Wilts.; Market Harborough, Leics.; Wootton Courtney, Som. (bosses):

Birds are a popular 'marginal' subject not only in manuscripts but in stained glass where they perform various antics and carry a wide range of utensils or implements in their claws e.g. Yarnton, Oxon.

Swan

BOAT see also *Ship, Nave.*
The roughly boat-shaped container for incense (q.v.) from which it is ladled with a small spoon into the censer or thurible. Symbolises prayer of the church. Boat is sometimes an attribute of apostles (q.v.)

BOOK
Attribute of Evangelists (q.v.), Doctors (q.v.) and sometimes Apostles (q.v.) also of Christ in Majesty (see Doom). In the former cases it symbolises the truth of the gospel while in the last it is the Book of Life (and Judgment).

Book

BOSS
Carved or sculptured projection at crossing of vault-ribs often bearing heraldic or symbolic device — see Roof.

Brass

BRASS

Monument in form of thin, engraved brass (alloy) plate indented into stone or marble slab (casement). The countersunk design (indent or matrix) in the casement often survives when the brass has been pilfered. Finest brasses date from C14 and the best collection is in Cobham, Kent. They provide a rich quarry for costume and armour as well as providing examples of symbolism e.g. Aldborough, Aughton, Burghwallis, Yorks.

BREAD

Symbolises the sustaining of life, God's Providence and also the Eucharist (often indicated by wheat and vine). Loaves of bread are sometimes an attribute of St. Phillip (see Apostles) and of St. Mary of Egypt e.g. Kenn, Devon (screen).

BURIAL   see also *Coffin.*

Mediaeval burial was normally in the ground (sometimes in vaults) and the corpse was often laid directly in the grave protected only by a shroud (which legally had to be of wool from 1678 to 1814. e.g. shroud brasses at Digswell, Herts). Only the rich had personal coffins of stone or wood, others made temporary use of the common or parish coffin. Graves were not owned and old bones were frequently disturbed when a grave was dug. Such disturbed remains were normally collected into a crypt or charnel-house. The bodies of those who died away from home were sometimes rendered down and only the bones brought back for interment (cf. Heart Burial). Suicides, excommunicates and those who died violently without absolution were denied Christian burial yet the burial of the dead was a Corporal Work of Mercy (q.v.). e.g. Feltwell, Norf. (bench end). Burial inside church was originally reserved for saints, important ecclesiastics and founders. Later 'table tombs' sometimes had recumbent effigies (see Monuments).

Skeleton in Shroud

BURSE

Stiffened and embroidered fabric envelope to contain the linen cloth (corporal) on which the chalice and paten were placed during Mass.

Mediaeval examples survive at Hessett, Suff.;
Wymondham, Norf.

CAIN
Adam's son, murderer of his brother Abel (Gen. 6)
traditionally with the jaw-bone of an ass e.g.
Irish crosses; Capel, Kent. (mural); Norwich
cathedral (boss); St. Neot, Cornw. (glass). The
sacrifice of Cain occurs: Framlingham, Suff.
(tomb); Salisbury cathedral (chapter-house
carving); St. Neot, Cornw. (glass) and his death:
Norwich cathedral (nave boss).

CALENDAR   see also *Kalendar*
The secular calendar was indicated by the Labours
of the Months (q.v.) and the Zodiac (q.v.). These
representations symbolised the labour resulting
from man's fallen state (Gen. 3.17-19) and
earthly existence as opposed to heavenly bliss
(see R.I.P.).

CANDLE   see also *Light: Paschal Candle*

Our Lady of the
taper

Symbol of celebration and joy – hence the
multiplication of lighted candles on great feasts
and the use of yellow (unbleached) candles at
Requiems. They also symbolise faith, witness
and self-sacrifice. They can also symbolise
Christ, the Light of the World, and the Christian
church (Rev. 1. 12ff.) In the Middle Ages
numerical grouping of candles had symbolic
significance: three for the Holy Trinity, four
for the Gospel Makers (Evangelists), Five for
the Sacred Wounds or for a Rosary chaplet
(Marian mystery), six for daily prayer, seven for
the Sacraments or Holy Spirit's Gifts, nine for
the angelic orders. Two represent the two
natures of Christ. The elaboration of candlesticks
derives from the symbolic and sacramental
nature of the candles. A C15 candlestick
survives at Holme, Notts. and a candelabra with
the Madonna and St. George at Bristol, Temple
church.

CANDLEMAS
Feast of the Purification BVM now renamed The
Presentation in the Temple (Feb. 2nd). Instituted
to replace similar pagan ceremony. Bede says
that by c. 700 A.D. the pagan lustrations round
fields which took place on this day had been

replaced by 'processions in which lighted candles are carried in memory of the Divine Light which has illuminated the world'. Nowadays the procession tends to be confined to church or reduced to congregation holding lighted candles at the Gospel which contains the words 'a light to lighten the Gentiles' (Lk. 2.32).

CANONISATION   see also *Saints*

The formal and public recognition of exemplary sanctity now given by Papal recognition but for a long time could be result of popular acclaim or local cult. The names of such persons are introduced into the central prayer of the Mass called the Canon.

CARVING

Enormous destruction but survivals in out-of-way places (bosses, misericords, tombs) well worth searching out as they illustrate many aspects of mediaeval life and thought e.g. Paignton, Devon where Kirkham chapel has statues of angels and saints, reliefs and recumbent effigies; Beverley minster, Yorks. has an even more impressive concentration on Percy tomb.

Carving

CASTLE   see also Elephant (s.v. *Animals*)

Heraldic rather than symbolic device.

CEILINGS AND VAULTINGS   see also *Roof*

Even when undecorated were given symbolic significance as representing 'the more unlearned servants of Christ . . . who adorn the Church, not by their learning, but by their virtues alone.' (Durandus).

Castle

CELURE

An ornate canopy, carved and coloured, set up to honour the Rood (q.v.) or the Sanctuary (q.v.) often decorated with carved emblems and gilded bosses. Survivals at Braughing, Herts.; Dummer, Hants.; Hennock, Ideford, King's Nympton, Devon; Lavenham, Suff.; North Cerney, Glos.; Southwold, Stowlangtoft, Suff. and modern examples are worth noting.

CHAIR

Most important is 'cathedra' or bishop's chair which gives status to cathedral. Symbolises

Chair

Chalice

teaching authority. Parish churches sometimes have a particularly elaborate chair for bishop's use when visiting. Interesting mediaeval chairs exist at: Beverley Minster, Yorks ('frith-stool' q.v.); Bishops Canning, Wilts. (monastic 'carrel' or study-chair with paintings, some identify it as confessional); Connington, Hunts. (abbot's chair from Peterborough); Great Dunmow, Essex (monastic chair now used in 'Flitch' ceremony for enthroning happily married couple); Jarrow St. Paul's, Durham (associated with Bede); Ripon cathedral ('frith-stool'); Sprotborough, Yorks. ('frith-stool'); Stanford Bishop, Herefs. (associated with St. Augustine); Westminster Abbey (coronation chair).

Many elaborate chairs currently found in sanctuary are post-Reformation and originally served a secular purpose but some (e.g. Combe Martin, Devon; Cartmel, Lancs.; Halsall, Lancs.; Ledbury, Herefs.; Sanderstead, Surrey) indicate by the carved symbolism that they were designed for ecclesiastical use.

CHALICE   see also *Vessels,* Altar
Ritual cup used for wine at Mass, Eucharist, Holy Communion. The Holy Grail was believed to be the cup used by Christ at the Last Supper. Chalice with a wafer (inscribed with monogram or cross) over it symbolises Holy Eucharist. It is an attribute of St. John the Evangelist and with paten or eucharistic wafer appears on coffin lids to indicate that occupant was a priest (chalice and paten often buried with them). Occurs on brasses: Cley-next-the-sea, Norf.; Clothall, Herts.; Gazeley, Suff.; Marsworth, Bucks.; Radwell, Herts.; Shorne, Kent; Wensley, Yorks.; York St. Michael Spurriergate.

Can be a symbol of Christ's agony (Mark 14.36) e.g. Windsor St. George, Berks. (stalls). Mediaeval chalices rarely survived as they were looted for their material value but some remain e.g. Combe Keynes, Dorset; Little Faringdon, Oxon.; Nettlecombe, Som., Wylye, Wilts.

CHANCEL
That part of the church beyond the nave (q.v.) which contains the quire (q.v.) and sanctuary (q.v.). Its name is derived from the open-work screens ('cancelli') which originally indicated the

Chancel

Chancel screen

division from the nave. Originally chancels were built on a slightly lower level than the nave to indicate clerical humility but most are now raised above nave level. The chancel is often out of alignment with the nave ('weeping chancel'). This has been interpreted as symbolising Christ's head drooping on the Cross. Most chancels incline to the North (as in iconography Christ's head leans towards His right shoulder) but a large minority veer towards the South. In spite of the mediaeval love of symbolism, this mis-alignment is probably not symbolic but results from changes in orientation (q.v.) due to the length of the building process (work usually started in Spring when the sun is just North of the equator). Other sources of discrepancy might include: the fixing of orientation on the point of sun-rise on the patronal festival, inaccuracy due to the cumulative effect of errors in the Julian calendar, or just bad laying-out due to the need to keep part of the church in use during the building or re-building process.

CHANCEL SCREEN

Wooden or stone partition between nave and chancel. Of all the features of the church, this one is pre-eminent in its universality and antiquity. The chancel screen in Western Europe is a close parallel to the Eastern iconostasis since it was originally closed to the roof, was occasionally veiled (as in Lent) and the images on its panels made it too a 'picture stand'. There is much symbolism in the carved details and surviving paintings of mediaeval screens which were originally surmounted by the great crucifix (rood) from which its alternative name of rood screen (q.v.) was derived. After the destruction associated with the Reformation, there were some fine replacements in the Stuart period e.g. Croscombe, Som.; Passenham, Northants.; Leeds St. John, Yorks.; Trentham, Staff.; Wimborne, Dorset; not to mention modern revivals.

CHANTRY

1. Endowment maintaining priest to chant Mass for founder or others after their death.
2. Chapel or altar so endowed. According to the size of the bequest chantries may partially

Chantry

support a priest at an altar or fully support several clergy and others together with a chapel or church (usually enclosing the tomb of the founder). Many chantries were corporate foundations in which the guilds were particularly involved. This institution rapidly developed after the terror of the Black Death (mid. C14) and the location of chantries affected church-planning as their altars were raised in aisles, before pillars, on tombs and in special extensions. As the chantry priest's duties ended with the singing of Mass and other prayers for the dead, chantries often took on other voluntary responsibilities: elementary education, maintenance of bridges, parochial work etc. (e.g. Grantham, Lincs.; Higham Ferrers, Northants.; Lavenham, Suff.; St. Ives, Hunts.; Wakefield, Yorks. Examples of small chantries: Ampton, Suff.; Berkeley, Glos.; Buckingham, Bucks.; Stoke Charity, Hants. has a reredos significantly depicting the Mass of St. Gregory (q.v.) Tiverton, Devon is richly decorated but perhaps the two finest are the Beauchamp tomb at Warwick St. Mary, Warks. and the Percy tomb in Beverley Minster, Yorks.

Sometimes special accommodation was provided for large groups of chantry priests e.g. Brympton D'Evercy, Som.; St. William's College, York.

CHAPEL
Small church or independent sub-division of larger church with its own altar. Derived from 'capella' (cloak) as first 'chapel' enshrined St. Martin's cloak at Tours. Chantry chapel: see above. Guild chapel: one supported and used by guild. Lady chapel: one dedicated to Virgin Mary ('Our Lady'). Mortuary chapel: for overnight accommodation of the dead.

CHERUB   see also *Angelic Orders*
Often reduced to a winged head. Appears on fonts, gravestones, other sculptures and on altar frontal at Alveley, Salop.

Cherub

CHESTS   see also *Aumbry*
Provided safekeeping for vestments, relics and other valuables. Many cathedrals possess cope-chests for flat storage of richly embroidered choir and processional vestment. Parochial

chests survive e.g. Alnwick, North. (carved), Brancepeth, Durham; Derby St. Peter, Derbys. (carving); Dersingham, Norf. (painting); Harty, Kent (carving); Newport, Essex (richly painted, may have doubled as occasional altar); Sheppey, Kent, Wath-by-Ripon, Yorks. (carvings).

CHI-RHO MONOGRAM see also *Initial Letters*

One of oldest Christian emblems, formed by abbreviation of 'Christ' by reducing to first two Greek letters. It appears in catacombs, was Constantine's 'victorious sign', occurs on ancient crosses and gravestones and is in continuing use. Mediaeval survivals are rare though there is a possibly C6 example on a carved stone at Treflys, Caernarvon, Wales.

Chi-Rho monogram

CHOIR see also *Quire*.

'The choir is so called from the harmony of the clergy in their chanting, or from the multitude collected at the Divine Offices. The word 'chorus' is derived from 'chorea' or from 'corona', for in early times they stood like a crown around the altar and thus sang the psalms in one body; but Flavianus and Theodorus taught the antiphonal method of singing, having received it from St. Ignatius (c. 100 A.D.) who himself learnt it by inspiration. The two choirs then typify the angels and the spirits of righteous men while they cheerfully and mutually spur each other on in this holy exercise.' (Durandus, who is not reliable on etymology but a veracious witness to a tradition which is as old as the Christian church.) Choir stalls face each other in two groups to facilitate antiphonal singing which was sometimes accompanied by a choir organ (the one at Ripon cathedral has a hand for beating time). The decoration of choir often includes angelic musicians.

CHRISMATORY

Container for the sanctified oils (q.v.) used in Christian ceremonies. It usually had three compartments. Mediaeval chrismatories have been found at Canterbury St. Martin, Kent; Granborough, Bucks.

Choir

Statue of Christ,
seated as Judge

Cruciform halo

St. Christopher
medal

CHRIST

'The anointed One' — prophet, priest and king.
Mediaeval representations commonly took one
of three forms:

Seated as Judge (see Doom, Majestas) e.g.
  Alfriston, Sussex; Llandanwg, Merion.;
  Widford, Herts.

Hanging on Cross (see Crucifixion, Rood). Most
  frequent in glass and not uncommon on
  brasses. Also on murals e.g. Beverstone, Glos.;
  Ely Deanery chapel, Cambs.

At His mother's bosom (see Epiphany, Madonna,
  Natitivity) often occurs in painting and
  stained glass. Rare example on brass at
  Cobham, Kent.

For the chief events of His earthly life see
Nativity, Infancy, Ministry, Passion, Resurrection,
Ascension. Christ's genealogy (see Jesse Tree)
occurs in Canterbury cathedral, Kent (glass).
Representations of Christ appear e.g. Breedon-
on-the-Hill, Leics. (C8/9 carvings); East Ham,
Essex (painting); East Wellow, Hants (painting);
Ely cathedral, Exeter cathedral, Gloucester
cathedral (bosses), Oddington, Glos. (painting);
Ottery St. Mary, Devon (boss); Swillington,
Staffs. (statue); Tewkesbury Abbey (boss).
Christ is always depicted with a cruciform halo
and with a cross and banner in Resurrection
scenes. Usually His wounds are shown e.g..
Plympton, Devon (screen) and He may raise
His right hand in blessing and hold a book in
His left. His emblems include a Cross and banner
e.g. Launcells, Poughill, Cornw. (bench-ends);
initials such as IHS, INRI and He may be
symbolised by fish, pelican, panther etc. See
also Arms of Christ, Initial Letters, Instruments
of Passion, Pity, Trade.

CHRISTOPHER, SAINT

The legendary Christopher was a giant wishing
to serve the most powerful king. After several
unsatisfactory vassalages, a hermit (q.v.)
persuaded him to use his strength in helping
travellers across a river. In this service he
eventually bore the Christ-child, a supernatural
burden, and became a Christian and,
subsequently, a martyr. He provides one of the
most conspicuous subjects of mediaeval church
art, generally on wall facing main entrance. He

typified the Third Estate or Common Man and
was patron of travellers and spiritual pilgrims.
The sight of his image was believed to be a
prophylactic against unprepared death. e.g.
Bradninch, Devon (screen); Breage, Cornw.
(mural); Fring, Norf. (mural); Mere, Wilts. (glass);
Morley, Derbys. (brass); Pickering, Yorks. (mural);
Shorewell, I.o.W. (mural); Stockerston, Leics.
(glass); Tattershall, Lincs. (brass); Terrington
St. Clement, Norf. (sculpture); Weeke, Hants.
(brass); Willingham, Cambs. (mural); Wood
Eaton, Oxon. (mural with prophylactic
inscription).

CHRISOMS
Erroneously identified as unbaptised infants. In
fact, term for baptised infants who died before
they were a month old and whose chrisom (see
Baptism) served as a shroud e.g. brasses at
Cranbrook, Teynham, Kent.

CHRONOGRAM
Inscription describing event dated by letters
with numerical value within inscription.
X or W = 10; U or V = 5; I or J = 1. A C15-16
device e.g. Brookthorpe, Glos. (porch);
Westminster Abbey (Ludovic Stuart tomb).

CHURCH AND SYNAGOGUE
The latter was seen as a type or aborted form of
the former and provided iconographic contrast in
the Middle Ages. Few survivals. e.g. Little
Casterton, Rutland (mural); Southrop, Glos.
(font).

CHURCH SYMBOLISM
Cruciform shape introduced as early as C5 and
other symbolic ideas were derived from
superseded Jewish Temple (Holy of Holies,
Holy Place, Outer Court), from Apocalyptic
images, and from the notion that the material
fabric of the building should mirror the nature
of the Church. The symbolism of the sanctuary
as heaven and the nave as earth was familiar in
early C5.

The nave is the ship (Lat. 'navis) of the
Church, the ark of salvation in a storm-tossed
world and its symbolic decoration is concerned
with the themes of time, work, temptation,

St. Christopher

35

deadly sins, life-giving faith, saving works, with struggle and decision in the Church militant.

The quire and sanctuary represent heaven: it is peopled with white-robed angels and saints and its life is drawn from and centred on the altar which is Christ. Much of its symbolism is derived from the imagery of the Apocalypse (q.v.).

The division between these two states is death, represented by the chancel-arch and screen surmounted by its towering rood which provides a safe bridge from this world to the next ('Pontifex', Latin for priest/bishop, means bridge-builder). Over the chancel arch was painted the Doom or Judgment, a reminder that time must have a stop, that this world is a vale of soul-making, and decisions in time have eternal consequences. A 'Doom' over the church porch emphasises the division of judgment between those within and without the Church whereas one in the interior tends to indicate a division between the spiritual and institutional Christians.

Sometimes, parts of a large church retain names such as Galilee, Jerusalem. One explanation is that these marked the locations of appropriate scenes in the mystery plays. Another is that they were substitutes for pilgrimages to the actual places in the Holy Land.

CHURCHYARD   see also *Burial, Coffin, Death, Lych-gate.*
'God's acre'. The enclosed ground around a church dedicated to Christian burial and whose sacred purpose is usually indicated by a churchyard cross (q.v.). The Southern half is usually more extensive than the North because the North symbolised the realm of evil (see Earth and Sky) and was ill-favoured and lay in shadow.

CIBORIUM
1. A cup-shaped vessel with a lid to hold consecrated wafers used at Holy Communion. A mediaeval example survives at Tong, Salop.

2. A cup shaped canopy to honour High altar and protect it from dust (see Altar Canopies). No ancient examples though there are modern ones e.g. Holbrook School chapel, Suff.

Clock

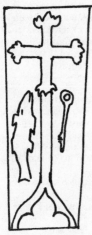

Coffin slab or lid

Coffin stools

CIRCLE, Ring
Symbol of a bond, and of eternity, and therefore especially of an eternal bond.

CLOCK see also *Bell; Dial, Mass; Hours.*
Great mediaeval churches often possessed an elaborate clock. It could symbolise order but Durandus saw it as 'teaching the diligence that should be in priests to observe at the proper times the Canonical Hours as He saith: "Seven times a day do I praise Thee" (Ps. 119.164)'.

COFFINS see also *Burial; Brasses.*
In C12–13 wealthy used shallowly buried stone coffins whose lids came level with the church-floor and similar flat slabs were used as monuments to those buried in the church-yard. These often bear an elaborate cross, incised or in relief, sometimes with emblems indicating the occupation of the deceased; weapons for soldiers; bow, axe or horn for foresters; chalice or pastoral staff for clergy; fish for fishmongers; a glove for glovers; shears for wool-merchant etc. An incised key usually indicates a steward or other office-holder. e.g. Bakewell, Derbys.; Bishopstone, Sussex; Cadney, Lincs.; Durham St. Oswald; Kirkoswald, Cumb.; Newcastle castle chapel, North.; Wareham, Dorset; Wirksworth, Derbys.; Winterbourne Basset, Wilts. Massive floor-slabs in bluish-grey stone with heraldic carving and low relief are called Ledger Stones and date C17–18. Iron gravestones occur in early iron-smelting areas e.g. Rotherfield, Wadhurst, Sussex.

COFFIN STOOLS
Used to support coffin at Lych-gate (q.v.) or in church e.g. Beddingham, Etchingham, Sussex.

COLOUR
Brightened almost every surface in mediaeval church: frescoes on walls, coloured and gilded statues, ironwork, ceilings and bosses; painted fonts and bench-ends, enamelled brasses, all heraldic devices properly limned, screen-panels with painted saints, coloured patterns on walls and arcades and windows filled with brilliant stained glass. Much of the colour was symbolic and appropriated to particular use: gold for God,

silver for angels, blue for Virgin Mary, green for life. Original dim work remains but there is an increasing tendency to restore or imitate original decoration e.g. Blisland, Cornw.; Cantley, Yorks.; Harberton, Devon; Thaxted, Essex; Harrogate St. Wilfrid (modern church).

COLOURS, LITURGICAL

The colours of vestments, church-hangings, frontals, veils etc. changed in accordance with nature of feast, ecclesiastical season and nature of service:

White: Confessors, Virgins, Angels, Easter, Ascension, Dedication, All Saints', Feasts of B.V.M. (sometimes blue).

Black: Good Friday, Requiems, Rogation Days, Lent, Advent.

Scarlet: Apostles, Evangelists, Martyrs, Feasts of Holy Spirit.

Green on ferial days (neither feast nor penitential).

Modern Catholic practice replaces black by violet (except Good Friday and Requiems), sometimes uses Rose on Mid-Lent Sunday and (where they exist) Gold vestments for major feasts when otherwise white or red would be used.

The symbolism is fairly obvious: white for purity, red for blood and fire, black or violet for mourning, green for life.

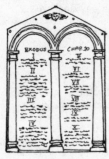

The Ten Commandments

COMMANDMENTS, TEN

Moral virtues were taught during the middle ages in catechism, symbols, sermons, illustrations of virtues, vices, and corporal works of mercy as well as through the Ten Commandments. The writing of these on vast boards began under Elizabeth I to fill the denuded spaces created by iconoclasm and whitewash and to further the notion that the much despoiled and modified buildings were still churches and concerned with moral behaviour e.g. Baddiley, Ches.; Bengeworth, Glos.; Gateley, Norf.; Lanteglos, Cornw.; Ludlow, Salop. Matching boards contained the Creed and Lord's Prayer e.g. Wistantow, Salop. This innovation represents not merely a change from Catholicism to Protestantism but an emphasis on religion communicated through the written word rather than through non-verbal symbols.

COMMUNION TABLE   see also *Altar*.

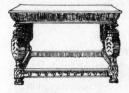

Communion table

Reformation substitute for Altar, symbolising change of emphasis in principal Christian service from sacrifice to communion. Some very fine examples from Stuart period e.g. Astbury, Chesh.; Beeston Regis, Norf.; Burlescombe, Devon; Halesworth, Suff.; Lutterworth, Leics.; Spetchley, Worcs.; Theddlethorpe All Saints, Lincs.; Whitwell I.o.W. Some of these were originally secular tables and with restoration of altars some have returned to a more or less secular use within the church.

COMMUNION OF SAINTS   see also *Saints*.

This credal article represents the reality of incorporation in Christ and the unity of all His members, living and dead. It is related to the notion of a three-fold church: on earth, militant; awaiting Heaven in Purgatory, expectant (Holy Souls); victorious saints in Heaven, triumphant. This conviction naturally led to prayers for the dead and prayers to the saints to aid their still struggling brethren. Remains of this awareness of an involved community that no man can number survive in glass, statuary, monuments and brasses.

COMPASSES

Long tradition of making compasses an attribute of God in His capacity as Creator. Blake's famous image has a long ancestry and some of its antecedants survive e.g. Norwich cathedral nave (boss); Malvern priory, Worcs. (boss); St. Neot, Cornw. (boss); York minster (Te Deum window). Corruption of 'God and Compasses' might explain inn-sign of 'Goat and Compasses'.

Compasses, usually accompanied by set-square, are an attribute of masons and found inscribed on their tombs (see Coffins).

Compass

CONFESSIONAL

The double or triple cupboards found in R.C. churches were introduced in C16. In the Middle Ages there was rarely any special structure for administering the Sacrament of Penance (q.v.) and confessions were heard from chancel-steps or behind chancel-screen. In some screens there are small apertures, possibly to facilitate this operation (see Rood Screen). Some churches had special 'shriving pews' abolished at the Reformation though one may survive at Bishops Canning, Wilts. There is an alleged stone confessional at West Tanfield, Yorks.

Domestic strife:
the sin of anger

CONFLICT   see also *Dragons.*

Fighting creatures sometimes symbolise the vice of Wrath e.g. bosses in Norwich cathedral cloisters; Sherborne, Dorset. Engagements between knights or between men and monsters may symbolise the 'Psychomachia', the continuing spiritual warfare between Virtue and Vice e.g. Ault Hucknall, Derbys.; Bolton, Westm. (tympana); Claverley, Salop, (mural); Lippitt, Devon (font); Long Marton, Westm. (tympanum). The same significance may be attached to wrestlers (q.v.).

Some churches have rare reminders of the mediaeval 'trial by combat' e.g. Canterbury cathedral (glass); Salisbury cathedral (Wyvil brass); Stowell, Glos. (mural). Compare 'Trial by water' (Canterbury, glass) and 'trial by fire' (York Minster glass).

Consecration
Cross

CONSECRATION   see also *Dedication.*

Originally only altars were concecrated. Practice extended to whole building in Dark Ages, probably due to re-use of pagan temples. The church must be fully endowed from goods lawfully acquired before the bishop 'alienates' it — puts it aside from profane use. The building is a symbol of the living church (the members of Christ) and its consecration has analogies with the services for marriage and for the reception of nuns. Twelve dedication crosses (q.v.), one for each article of the Creed, were painted or cut on both interior and exterior walls. These were anointed with oil as badges of Christ, stamping the building with His mark. Castor, Northants. has inscription recording its consecration in 1124, cf. Ashbourne, Derbys.; Jarrow St. Paul, Durham; Old Clee, Lincs.

CORBEL

Protruding wall-stone to carry beam. Often carved with symbols of virtues on south wall

with antithetical deadly sins on north. Other
subjects include angels, demons, evangelistic
symbols and heads of contemporaries: kings,
nobles, prelates, donors and even self-portrait
of the carver e.g. Beverley St. Mary, Yorks.;
Daglinworth, Glos.; Kilpeck, Herefs.; Luffingham,
Rutland.; Sompting, Sussex; Westbere, Kent.

CORN DOLLY

Humanoid figure made from last sheaf of
harvest. Pagan origin: dwelling of corn-spirit
during winter. They occupied a place of honour
at Harvest Festival and were taken into church.
Recently still placed in porches: Bewley,
Overbury, Worcs. Other symbolic thank-
offerings include the garland of flowers or
holly which sometimes still decorates church-
tower.

CORONATION B.V.M.   see also *Rosary*.

The coronation of Christ's mother after her
assumption (q.v.) is the archetypal symbol
of the heavenly reward for those who have
fulfilled God's will on earth. e.g. Adlingfleet,
Yorks. (porch); Quenington, Glos. (tympanum);
Ripon, Yorks. (alabaster); Stanford, Northants.
(glass); Sutton Bingham, Som. (mural);
Tewkesbury, Glos. (glass).

Coronation B.V.M.

CORPORAL WORKS OF MERCY

Derived from Matt. 25.35ff.: giving food to the
hungry, drink to thirsty, hospitality to
strangers, clothing to naked, ministering to sick
and prisoners. To these six good works a seventh
was added after C12, of burying the dead
(Tobit 1.16ff) e.g. Combs, Suff. (glass); Feltwell,
Norf. (bench-end); York All Saints' (glass).
Mercy (pity, fellow-feeling) is often personified
as a woman.

CREATION   see also *Compasses*.

Windows depict the works of the seven days of
creation (Gen. 1) at e.g. Malvern Priory, Worcs.;
St. Neot, Cornw. The end of the world is figured
in York All Saints (glass) — see also Doom.

Credence

CREDENCE

Ecclesiastical 'sideboard' in chancel on which
vessels and materials for Mass are placed in

readiness e.g. Fyfield, Berks.; Winchester St. Cross, Hants. Credence shelves occur in recess of piscina (q.v.) e.g. Dersingham, Norf.; Kirk Hallam, Derbys.; Litchfield, Hants.; Millom, Cumb.; Skelton, Yorks.; Stanford, Berks.; Trumpington, Cambs.; Woodford, Northants.; Yatton, Som. There are fine wooden credence tables from the Stuart period e.g. Battle, Sussex; Cobham, Surrey; Chipping Warden, Northants.; Islip, Oxon.

CREED, APOSTLES'

From C4 at least, the baptismal creed of Western church and outline of catechetical and other instruction. Traditionally, one clause was attributed to each apostle. In the fully developed iconographical scheme each apostle was balanced by a prophet who 'foretold' that particular contribution, thus:

Prophecy	Image	Apostle
Jeremiah (3.9; 32.17)	God enthroned	Peter: I believe in God .... earth
David (Ps. 2.7)	Christ enthroned	Andrew: and in J.C. our Lord
Isaiah (7.14)	Nativity	James Gt.: conceived ... born of V.M.
Zechariah (7.10)	Crucifixion	John: suffered .. crucified .. buried
Amos (9.6)	Ascension	James Less: ascended ... Almighty
Malachi (3.5)	Second Coming	Phillip: from thence .... dead
Joel (2.28)	Pentecost	Bartholomew: I believe in Holy Ghost
Zephaniah (3.9)	Catholic Church	Matthew: the Holy Catholic Church
Malachi (2.16)	Penance	Simon: the forgiveness of sins
Ezekiel (37.12)	General Resurrection	Jude: the resurrection of the dead
Daniel (12.2)	Coronation of Virgin	Matthias: the life everlasting. Amen.

The scheme is not always complete. There are some variations but the imagery is found everywhere: on fonts (q.v.), in glass (Fairford, Glos.; Malvern Priory, Worcs.), on screens (Barton Turf, Norf.; Bovey Tracey, Bradninch,

Chudleigh, Ipplepen, Kenton, Devon; Southwold,
Suff.; Stoke Gabriel, Devon), pulpit (Long
Sutton, Som), roof (Bere Regis, Dorset), mural
(Smarden, Kent – 12 articles associated with
Instruments of Passion (q.v.)); stalls (Astley, Warks.).

After the Reformation the Creed, together
with the Lord's Prayer and Ten Commandments,
(q.v.), was ordered to be painted on boards
(usually located in chancel) e.g. Lambourne,
Sussex; Tivetshall St. Margaret, Norf.

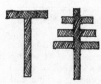

Tau cross   Papal
cross

CROSS   see also *Anglo-Saxon Cross;
Crucifix; Rood.*
A 'natural' symbol: four cardinal points (cosmic
significance), cross-roads (decision, crisis,
choice), being crossed (frustration, adversity,
fate), stick figure of a man. It is even more
'charged' as a Christian symbol: humiliation,
suffering, moral and actual burden (the product
of human handiwork) but, above all, of
redemption and triumph through supernatural
love. Among the ancient Egyptians, the Tau
(T-shaped) Cross was a symbol of eternity as the
looped-cross (ankh) was a symbol of life.
Christian examples are rare before C4 though
there appears to have been a cross shrine at
Pompeii. Symbolic and heraldic forms of the
cross are extremely numerous in the Middle
Ages. The Tau cross is an attribute of St.
Anthony and associated with life's pilgrimage
e.g. Curdworth, Warks. (mural), the Maltese
cross occurs in Norman sculpture, often
enclosed in a circle e.g. Wold Newton, Yorks.,
the Celtic cross is also often encircled and may
originally, like the Swastika, have associations
with sun worship. The cross rising from three
steps which symbolise faith, hope and charity
is called a 'calvary' e.g. Shouldham, Norf.,
while a cross whose arms terminate in points is
called a cross of suffering. A 'cross fleurie' has
elaborated terminals and St. Andrew's cross is a
saltire. The 'Greek cross' has equal arms, the
'Latin' a longer upright. A patriarchal cross has
two cross pieces, one longer than the other
whereas a papal cross has three.

Crosses were incised on coffin-lids (q.v.)
and some designs are of great beauty. They
also occur on brasses, sometimes with the figure
or head of the deceased placed on or within

Patriarchal cross

Cross of   Maltese
suffering   Cross

Greek cross

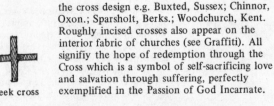

Greek cross

Calvary

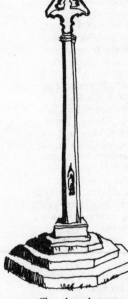

Latin cross

Churchyard cross

the cross design e.g. Buxted, Sussex; Chinnor, Oxon.; Sparsholt, Berks.; Woodchurch, Kent. Roughly incised crosses also appear on the interior fabric of churches (see Graffiti). All signifiy the hope of redemption through the Cross which is a symbol of self-sacrificing love and salvation through suffering, perfectly exemplified in the Passion of God Incarnate.

CROSS: ALTAR AND PROCESSIONAL

The Cross on the Altar (q.v.) is perhaps oldest church ornament. It symbolises the unity between the sacrifice of Christ and Mass and Holy Communion.

The Processional Cross (which in the Middle Ages sometimes consisted of attaching the altar cross to a pole) is a symbol of Christ and of faith, providing the banner behind which His church marches. Mediaeval examples survive at Durham St. Oswald; Lamport, Northants.; Thurnham, Lancs.

CROSS, CHURCHYARD   see also
Anglo-Saxon Cross.

Some may mark a Christian site antedating the building of the church e.g. Bewcastle, Cumb.; Whalley, Lancs. Later they indicated a location for preaching (I Cor. 1.23) and provided a 'station' for processions on Palm Sunday, Corpus Christi and Rogationtide. Occasionally, they have a receptacle for the monstrance (q.v.) e.g. Great Malvern, Worcs. They were usually surmounted by an elaborate crucifix which was usually destroyed at the Reformation and later occasionally replaced by a sundial e.g. Tilston, Ches.

Selected examples: Ampney Crucis, Glos.; Bitterley, Salop.; Checkley, Staffs.; Drayton, Som.; Eyam, Derbys.; Halton, Heysham, Lancs.; Ilam, Staffs.; Iron Acton, Glos.; Laleston, Glam.; Ripley, Yorks.; Rocester, Staffs.; Sherburn-in-Elmet, Yorks.

CROSS, CREEPING TO THE

A somewhat extravagant name for the individual and corporate veneration of the Cross which forms part of the Good Friday liturgy. The Cross is approached with three genuflections and kissed. The church cross is

normally venerated with a bow cf.:
'What time thou passest by the Rood, bow
humbly evermore
But not the Rood, but Him who there was
crucified, adore.'

Consecration cross

External
consecration cross

CROSS: DEDICATION OR CONSECRATION
see also *Consecration*.
Many survivals both on exterior and interior walls
e.g. Arundel, Sussex; Ashampstead, Berks.;
Ashmansworth, Hants.; Bapchild, Kent;
Berkeley, Glos.; Bures, Suff.; Climping, Sussex;
Crosthwaite, Cumb.; Great Canfield, Essex;
Kingston, Cambs.; Kirkstead, Lincs.; Moorlinch,
Som.; Ottery St. Mary, Devon.; Ovington, Norf.;
Potterne, Wilts.; Throcking, Herts.; Uffington,
Berks.; Westham, Sussex; Wisley, Surrey.

CROSS, ELEANOR
Erected by Edward I in 1291–4 to mark the
resting places of his wife's coffin as it was
conveyed from Harby, Notts. to Westminster.
Symbol of love and faith e.g. Geddington,
Hardingstone, Northampton, Northants.

CROWN   see also *Instruments of Passion*.
Golden: symbolises (*a*) earthly rule e.g. in
    representations of kings (*b*) martyrdom.
Thorn: Christ's passion, amendment for sins
    of thought, often borne by angel e.g.
    Furneaux Pelham, Herts.

CRUCIFIX
From C6 to C11 Christ was portrayed as
enthroned on the Cross, robed as priest or
king, sometimes wearing a royal crown and
without naturalistic signs of suffering. The
arms were outstretched horizontally as though
to embrace the world. The drooping, agonising
Christ develops as the later Middle Ages became
increasingly obsessed with suffering and death.
Reforming iconoclasm destroyed most
representations but there are survivals in glass,
particularly east windows which doubled as a
reredos (q.v.) e.g. Eaton Bishop, Herefs.;
Stockerston, Leics.; Wells cathedral; Winscombe,
Som.
Other examples: Auckland St. Andrew, Durham
(Anglo-Saxon cross); Coddenham, Suff.

Crucifix

(alabaster); Daglinworth, Glos. (panel, Saxon); Norwich cathedral (nave boss); Southfleet, Kent (brass); Wiston, Suff.; Winsham, Som. (panel).

CRUETS AND FLAGONS   see also *Credence*

Two stoppered vessels, for wine and water respectively, formed an invariable part of eucharistic plate from the earliest times. These cruets were usually of gold, silver or pewter though a mediaeval glass one was discovered at Lapworth, Warks. in C19. The mixing of a little water with wine before drinking was a classical practice and presumably used by Christ. Symbolically it was related to John 19.34 and I John 5.6,8 and also to the Incarnation. As the priest adds water to the wine he prays that we may be united to Christ's Divinity as He took on our humanity.

Flagon

Cruets appear as attribute of saints in minor or deacon's orders (e.g. St. Vincent). Occasionally a perforated spoon or strainer was used to remove impurities from the mixed chalice e.g. Dallington, Northants.; Diss, Norf.; Ramsbury, Wilts.

When the Reformation restored the chalice to the laity a larger wine container was required – the flagon e.g. Cirencester, Rendcombe, Glos.; Sudbury, Derbys.; Weston Zoyland, Som.

CRYPT

Originated in the catacombs and was called 'Confessio', 'Martyrium' or 'Memoria' when an oratory was built over a saint's resting-place. When this was replaced by a church, the High altar was located over the crypt-tomb. When a church did not have this origin a crypt was often provided to house relics e.g. Hexham, North.; Lastingham, Yorks.; Oxford St. Peter in the East; Ripon, Yorks. Crypts were also used as bone-houses (ossuaria) – see Burial, e.g. Hythe, Kent; Rothwell, Northants. Durandus says that crypts symbolise 'hermits who are devoted to the solitary life'. Parish churches with crypts include: Bamborough, North.; Berkswell, Warks.; Bosham, Sussex; Chillingham, North.; Newark, Notts.; Repton, Derbys.; Shillington, Beds.; Wing, Bucks.; Yeovil, Som.

Crypt

DANCE

In Christianity, as in Judaism (II Sam. 6.14;

Ps. 149.3), there is a tradition of sacred dance but, unfortunately, it is much attenuated. There was dancing in church and some have seen a slow dance in the movement of the Liturgy. Dancing in the churchyard was more unrestrained and frowned upon by the authorities because of its pagan associations and occasion for lewdness. The maypole often remains in church custody in spite of the Puritans and customary dances associated with church festivals (usually Whitmonday as a symbol of life and the gifts of the Spirit) persist e.g. Bampton, Oxon.; Goathland, Yorks.; Headington, Oxon.; Long Marston, Warks.; Overton, Hants.; Padstow, Cornw.

Dance:
violinist kissing
dancer

DANCE OF DEATH   see also *Memento Mori*.

'Oft cometh death among men. Though a man be in good point at eve, it can happen that he be dead by morrow.' This theme, with the emphasis that Death is no respecter of persons, became increasingly dominant in C14–15. It is represented in art, dance, drama, literature, mime and sermon and probably found its general origin in mendicant preaching though the specific reference to Death's Dance seems to stem from a late C14 French poem e.g. Boxgrove, Sussex (chantry carving); Hexham, North. (panel painting); Newark, Notts. (chantry painting); Norwich St. Andrew (glass); Sparham, Norf. (painted panel); Widford, Oxon. (painting); Windsor St. George, Berks. (misericord). The unexpectedness of death is also a theme in C14 'Pricke of Conscience' (York All Saints, glass).

Skeleton and
cardinal

DANCE OF SALOME

(Mk. 6.21-28). The proximate cause of John the Baptist's death. Symbolises sensual and emotional response v. spiritual and intellectual principles. In mediaeval art Salome is depicted as a 'tumbler' e.g. Chalfont St. Giles, Bucks. (mural); Chalgrove, Oxon (mural); Idsworth, Hants. (mural); Kingston Lisle, Berks. (mural); Norwich cathedral (cloister boss).

DAUGHTERS OF GOD   see *Virtues*.

DAVID, KING   see also *Harp, Jesse Tree, Prophets.*
Prophet, psalmist, righteous king, penitent, ancestor and type of Christ. e.g. Darenth, Kent (font); Exeter cathedral (boss); Leominster, Herefs. (mural); Lincoln cathedral (boss); Margaretting, Essex (glass); Newport, I.o.W. (mural); Norwich cathedral (boss); Westminster Abbey (boss); Worcester cathedral (boss); York All Saints, (glass).

Burial

DEATH   see also *Burial, Chantry, Dance of, Doom, Hatchment, Hearse, Memento Mori, Soul, Three Living.*
The Middle Ages did not seek to hide the fact of inevitable death. On the contrary, they delivered constant reminders of its significance. In the business of dying it was all important to make a good end. Man was a sinner and corruptible but repentance was possible and eternal life attainable. The contemplation of death was a powerful antidote to Pride, Sensuality and other false values. Death and the Maiden cogently contrasted temporal and eternal goods (murals at Alveley, Salop.; Padbury, Bucks.). An early C17 bell at Yetminster, Dorset is inscribed:
> 'I sound to bid the sick repent
> In hope of life when breath is spent.'

Consecration cross

DEDICATION OF CHURCH   see also *Consecration, Marian Dedications.*
Every church is dedicated directly and solely to God (the word 'church' means 'God's House') but individual churches are distinguished by their secondary dedication to a Christian saint or mystery. The Dedication Festival commemorates the day of dedication or consecration; Patronal Festival especially honours the saint to whom the church is dedicated; Feast of Title is the same thing when the church is dedicated to a mystery such as the Holy Cross, Ascension, Christ the King, Assumption etc.
　　　Dedications fall into three classes:
Memorial: churches erected on the site of martyrdom or burial of a saint.
Proprietary: churches dedicated to their founder. Particularly common in Celtic areas e.g. Cornwall, Wales.

Personal: reflecting interest or special devotion
of founder or patron (whether individual or
corporate). This last class greatly outnumbers
the other two combined.

Dedications afford clues to missionary activity,
popular cults and pilgrim routes. By far the
commonest dedication is to Our Lady, St. Mary
the Virgin. Such Mediaeval dedications number
well over two thousand. The next commonest,
at over twelve hundred, is to All Saints, closely
followed by St. Peter, with St. Michael in
fourth place with nearly nine hundred.

Demon

DEMONS

Besides the generalised hosts of Hell led by the
fallen archangel, Satan, mediaeval preaching
provided names and functions for particular
demons or devils, some original and some
translated from pagan or non-Christian religions.
Tutivillius (q.v.) is the only named demon whose
name and activities were generally familiar.
Demons are sometimes represented with a face
in their belly (see Grotesques). The function of
demons was to tempt, terrify and record sins
during this life and at its end to carry away lost
souls to Hell e.g. Cartmel, Lancs. (misericord);
Charlton Mackrell, Som. (bench-end); Gresford,
Denbighs. (misericord); Ludlow, Salop.
(misericord); Norwich cathedral (boss); Windsor
St. George, Berks. (misericord); York Minster
(tomb-slab).

The Devil

DEVIL, THE　　see also 'Horny, Old.'

Satan, the fallen archangel Lucifer, was normally
portrayed in the Middle Ages as a hideous monster
or as the 'great dragon' of the Apocalypse who is
overcome by St. Michael (q.v.) e.g. Fairford,
Glos. (East window). The Latin version of
Ps. 91.13 speaks of treading on the adder and
basilisk and treading underfoot the lion and the
dragon, consequently these creatures are used to
symbolise four aspects of the devil. e.g. Cartmel,
Lancs. (misericord); York St. Michael
Spurriergate (glass). The attributes of Satan and
his underlings are symbolical: horns for pride,
bear-toothed for manslaughterers, lion-clawed
for envy and covetousness, swollen-bellied for
gluttony, rotten spines for lechery, mutilated
feet for sloth (see Sins, Seven Deadly).

49

Scratch dials

DIALS: MASS, SCRATCH
Simple sundials were placed on plastered
exteriors, usually near the main entrance which
was normally the South door or porch. These
may survive as an incised circle with a central
hole (which once held the gnomon) and a
number of radii. Some divide the day into four
'tides' of three hours each, equivalent to the
Roman watches, corresponding to the Liturgical
'hours' (q.v.) e.g. Daglingworth, Glos.; Kirkdale,
Yorks. Usually they indicate the time of Mass,
Vespers (Evensong) and noon. Where more times
than these are indicated, Mass-time is shown by
a cross-bar (Broadwas, Stoulton, Worcs.) or a
thicker line (Farmington, Glos.). Other examples:
Climping, Sussex; Droxford, Hants.; Marsh
Baldon, Oxon.; Stockton, Wilts.

DIVINE OFFICE
The 'sacred duty' incumbent upon a priest to
say Mass daily and to recite the Hours (q.v.).
The usual time of the daily Mass was 9 a.m.

DIVES
The 'rich man' in the Lazarus story (Luke
16.19ff.), archetype of pleasure in this world
and pain in the next with Lazarus representing
the converse. This story was often associated
with Doom (q.v.) and Corporal Works (q.v.). This
mediaeval moral exemplar survived the
Reformation and poorer houses, even in C17,
often had painted hangings illustrating this story.
e.g. Ulcombe, Kent (mural); York Minster
(grave slab).

St. Jerome

DOCTOR
In Middle Ages retains its etymological meaning
of 'teacher' with associations of 'accredited' and
'authoritative'. The degree of Doctor qualified its
holder to teach in any university or school in
Western Europe. The 'Doctors of the Church' are
the great theologians who, in the West, were
exemplified by St. Ambrose (339–397),
St. Jerome (342–420), St. Augustine (354–430)
and the pope St. Gregory (540–604). Their
figures are carved or painted on pulpits;.
Burnham Norton, Norf.; Trull, Som.; appear on
rood-screens:Bradninch, Holne, Devon.; and

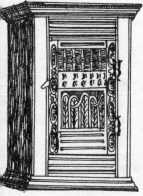

Dole cupboard

Donor

Doom

alternate with knights on the Bruce cenotaph at Guisborough, Yorks.

DOLE CUPBOARD

One of the mediaeval 'Corporal Works' (q.v.) was later institutionalised into a bread 'dole' financed by a parish benefactor or benefactors. This bread was given out at the end of church service, attendance at which (where possible) was a condition of donation. In C17 special cupboards, with ventilation openings in the doors, provided storage for this bread. Examples survive, sometimes containing hymn books, e.g. West Chiltington, Sussex.

DONORS

Benefactors who gave church furnishings sometimes sought a little publicity for their good works by inscriptions, heraldry (arms or rebus) or other emblematic representation e.g. Soberton, Sopley, Hants. (tower and porch); Syston, Leics. (tower). They may also appear as small figures kneeling in the corners of windows or murals. Such donors were often wealthy individuals but they may have been guilds or other corporations and there is evidence of joint effort by less exalted parishioners e.g. St. Neot, Cornw. where, in early C16, windows were severally presented by the 'wives', 'sisters' and 'young men'. The roof-bosses at Croscombe, Som. may represent donors but the identifying or petitionary scrolls have lost their lettering. Donors also appear on bench-ends at Milverton, Som. and Warkworth, Northants. and, more ostentatiously, at Tiverton, Devon.

DOOM   see also *Majestas*.

The Last Judgment was very frequently presented in sculpture, painting and glass. As a wall-painting it was usually placed round the chancel-arch which symbolically separated earthly from heavenly life. These representations represented in vivid, and often horrifying, detail the separation of the saved from the damned, the righteous from the unrighteous. The aim was didactic: to arouse the imagination and motivate by reward and punishment. e.g. murals: Chaldon, Surrey; Checkendon, Oxon.; Coombe, Oxon.; Dauntsey, Wilts.; Oddington, Glos.; Patcham,

51

Sussex; Penn, Bucks.; Salisbury St. Thomas, Wilts.; Wenhaston, Suff.; Symington, Beds.

DOOR

Door

The Door is Christ (John 10.9) and the symbolism of church doors accentuates this fact e.g. Fishlake, Yorks.; Tiverton, Totnes, Devon. In Romanesque churches the tympanum over the chief door was enriched with carvings on this theme:

Christ in Majesty, often with symbols of the Evangelists e.g. Elkstone, Glos.; Patrixbourne, Kent; Pedmore, Worcs.

Christ coming with angels in judgment e.g. Essendine, Rutl.; Rowlstone, Heref.; Water Stratford, Bucks.

Christ in the Virgin's arms e.g. Fownhope, Herefs.; Inglesham, Wilts.; Oxford Great St. Mary.

Christ harrowing Hell e.g. Beckford, Worcs.; Quenington, Glos.; Shobdon, Herefs. Common symbols over the door are the Agnus Dei (q.v.) and an incised cross (more than forty examples of each) e.g. Stanton Lacy, Salop. Much less common is a formalised Tree (q.v.) which represents both the tree of knowledge and the tree of the Cross e.g. Dinton, Bucks.

Apostles and saints could also help in the approach to God, hence the niche for their statue over many porches. The saints most commonly associated with church doors seem to be St. Michael (e.g. Hallaton, Leics.; Moreton Vallence, Glos.) or St. George (e.g. Brinsop, Herefs.), both suggesting that heavenly aid is available in the universal and continuing conflict with the Dragon (q.v.). Their 'guardianship' of the door might suggest a sort of frontier war, compare gargoyles and grotesques.

DOOR, DEVIL'S

Door on North side of nave which was supposed to be left open at Baptism for the escape of exorcised evil. There is no evidence for this whereas there is evidence of its convenience as a processional way.

Door knocker

DOOR KNOCKER

In important churches probably connected with the right of Sanctuary (q.v.) and therefore elaborated. It might also symbolise the power of prayer (Matt. 7.7ff.) e.g. Adel, Yorks.; Cound, Salop.; Dormington, Herefs.; Durham cathedral; Stogursey, Som.; Warboys, Hunts.; York All Saints Pavement. A boss at Bury St. Edmunds St. Mary may portray the sanctuary knocker of the destroyed abbey.

DRAGONS, WORMS, SERPENTS   see also *Monsters.*

Dragon

The serpent (snake) is an aboriginal symbol of evil and chaos but the Christian sources lie in Genesis and the Apocalypse and the Dragon is a preferred symbol to the snake which, biting its tail, can be a symbol for eternity and, sloughing its skin, of baptismal regeneration e.g. Ashover, Derbys. (font). Dragons are a general symbol of evil and of Satan himself. They appear on corbels, capitals, bosses and, as gargoyles and grotesques, on roofs and pinnacles e.g. Dover, Kent; Iffley, Oxon. They peer from foliage, whisper in human ears, attack humans or other monsters, are associated with St. Michael and St. George and, occasionally, might have literary reference. They may have been transferred from the great 'worms' of Scandinavian mythology e.g. Kilpeck, Herefs.

The conflict between the Lion (Christ) and the Dragon (Satan) is a common theme e.g. bosses: Canterbury, Lincoln, Norwich, Tewkesbury, Winchester, Worcester, York. Dragons also appear on misericords at Cartmel, Manchester, Lancs.; in the roof at Edenham, Lincs. and on the font at Stow, Lincs.

DRAMA

Jesus with doctors in the temple

Mediaeval drama had its roots in the liturgy, which was itself a dramatic act, and developed into miracle, morality and mystery plays which appear to have been performed in every town, usually by the guilds. Even some villages are known to have their own play and sometimes a natural theatre for its performance. Miracle plays deal with the legends of the saints with strong emphasis on the miraculous element; morality plays are concerned with the personification of virtues and vices (e.g. Everyman) while mystery plays centre on the mysteries of salvation: Christ's redeeming work, its anticipation in the Old Testament and the consummation of all things at Doomsday. Such plays in general, but particularly the last type, provided a powerful influence in the shaping of religious art and imagery.

EARTH AND SKY SYMBOLS   see also *Zodiac*.

Arms of St. Wilfred

Earth – represented by orb which, when surmounted by cross, refers to reign of Christ. Besides zooshpere, earth may symbolise Church.

East – source of sun and light = truth. Facing east symbolises search for light of truth (see also Orientation).

Fire – Holy Spirit, torments of Hell. Fire sometimes personified as monster vomiting flames (compare salamander s.v. Fabulous Beasts).

Garden – earthly or heavenly Paradise. The setting for love. Garden enclosed: Virgin Mary.

Light – Christ (John 8.12).

North – cold and night, heathendom. Reading Gospel from North side of altar symbolises church's mission to unconverted.

Rainbow – union, reconciliation (Gen. 9.12f.). In Doom (q.v.) it appears over Throne of God (Rev. 4.3).

Rivers, like water, (q.v.) represent life. The four rivers of Paradise symbolise the Gospels.

South – light and warmth, associated with N.T. Epistle read from South side of the altar represents the Bible instructing and comforting the church.

Stars – guidance to Christ (see Magi). Seven stars are associated with Christ (Rev. 1.19) e.g. Norwich cloister boss – probably refer to Spirit which He sent. Virgin is represented as crowned with twelve stars (Rev. 12.1). Saint with star on forehead is Dominic. A single star occurs at Tewkesbury (boss).

Sun and Moon – attributes of Virgin Mary (Rev. 12.1). On representation of Crucifixion symbolise witness of whole material creation. Saint with sun on breast is Thomas Aquinas. 'Sun in its spendour' is badge of House of York.

Sun and Moon

Well or Fountain – life, rebirth, baptism, eternal life. Christ's wounds sometimes represented as wells. Sealed well or fountain – Virgin Mary.

West — darkness, evil, abode of demons and of
the Prince of Darkness.

Wings — divine mission. Attribute of angels and
of evangelistic symbols.

EASTER SEPULCHRE

Easter Sepulchre

Symbol of garden tomb from which Christ rose.
Usually located on North side of chancel and
consists of richly canopied recess to
accommodate the Host and Altar crucifix
during the period of fast and vigil from Good
Friday to Easter Day (sometimes a table-tomb
doubled for this purpose). Its panels are carved
with figures of the soldiers at the tomb and a
representation of the Resurrection. These
sepulchres were decorated with flowers and
candles and parishioners maintained a continual
watch (Mark 14.34.37) as in contemporary
Catholic 'altar of repose'. e.g. Arnold, Notts.;
Bampton, Oxon,; Cowthorpe, Yorks.; Darlington,
Durham; Hawton, Notts.; Heckington, Lincs.;
Navenby, Lincs.; Northwold, Norf.; Owston,
Yorks.; Patrington, Yorks.; Wythybrook, Warks.

EMBLEMS AND ATTRIBUTES

An emblem is alternative to direct portrayal
whereas attribute identifies an image but has no
individual significance (thus a pig with a monkish
figure indicates St. Anthony of Egypt but a
pig alone would not do so).

Emblems of Christ: Agnus Dei, Chi-Rho,
IES, IHS, Fish, Instruments of Passion, Five
Wounds.

Emblems of Virgin Mary: Arma Virginis, Lily,
crowned M, MR.

Indicators of other saints are either generic
(cleric, martyr) or specific (i.e. attribute).
Vestments indicate clergy and distinguish bishop,
priest, deacon, acolyte while habit shows that
the representation is of a monk, friar, hermit etc.
Martyrs carry pointers to the manner of their
death: Paul a sword, Stephen stones, Sebastian
arrows, Lawrence a gridiron. A book is
appropriate to evangelists, doctors, founders of
religious orders and the very learned (e.g.
Catherine of Alexandria). A chalice may be
generic of priests but specific in the cases of John
the Evangelist, Barbara, Benedict, Richard of
Chichester. A church held in the hand usually

Emblem

distinguishes the founder of a church or of a religious order. A cross on the end of a long staff belongs to a missionary preacher. Specific attributes include Blaise's comb, Catherine's wheel, Barbara's tower, Clement's anchor, Hugh's swan. The most general ones are the virgin's lily and the martyr's palm. Saints who have not acquired a specific attribute are given a generic one with sometimes an identifying scroll.

Emblems and attributes associated with Christian mystery, holy life and heroic death invested everyday objects with profound significance and provided common life with constant reminders of absolute values.

ENTRY INTO JERUSALEM see also *Palm Sunday*.

Symbolises short-lived nature of earthly triumph, the fickleness of mankind, the emptiness of general popularity. The frequent depiction of this event is probably an indication of the impact of the dramatic and elaborate ceremonies of Palm Sunday e.g. Aston Eyre, Salop. (tympanum); Higham Ferrers, Northants. (door); West Haddon, Northants. (font).

EPIPHANY see also *Magi*.

The 'manifestation' of God in Christ. Modern emphasis is on the 'showing forth' to the Gentiles, symbolised by the Magi but traditionally the festival celebrated two additional manifestations; the Divine Mission (Christ's Baptism) and Divine Power (miracle at Cana). Epiphany, Jan. 6th., is 'Twelfth Night' (and end of Christmas festivities) and 'Old Christmas Day'. Dec. 25th was a Roman introduction of C4 to abrogate a sun festival.

EPISCOPAL THRONE see *Chair*.

EPITAPHS

Mediaeval grave inscriptions are rare and restricted to Memento Mori (q.v.) and requests for prayers, typified in:

'Whosoe'er thou art that passeth here
Remember I am what you will be
And was what you are; therefore pray for me.'

(East Horsley, Surrey).

MY·FRIENDS·SO
DEAR·AS·YOV·PAS
BY·SOE·AS·YOV·ARE
SOE·ONC·WAS·I
AND·AS·I·AM
SOE·SHALL·YOV·BE

Epitaph

A less usual sentiment is implied in:

> 'Henry Nottingham and his wife lie here
> That made this church's steeple and quire
> Two sets of vestments and peal of bells also.
> Therefore may Christ save them from woe
> And bring their souls to bliss in heaven
> By your prayers of Pater and Ave gently sung.'
>
> (Holme, Norf.)

Requests for prayers cease after the Reformation and the note of self-praise rises to a crescendo on grandiloquent monuments and inscriptions.

EVANGELISTS, THE FOUR

St. Matthew, St. Mark, St. Luke and St. John — the traditional Gospel makers. They may be symbolised by a square or the number four. Other possible symbols: the four life-giving rivers of Paradise, the arms of the Cross centrifugally spreading the Good News which the cross bears at its centre. They occupy the tower pinnacles at Gayton, Norf.

EVANGELISTS' EMBLEMS

Derived from Rev. 4.7 (cf. Ezekiel 1.10).) Matthew begins with Christ's human genealogy — winged man. Mark opens with a voice crying in the wilderness — winged lion. Luke introduces the sacrifice of Zecharias — winged ox. John soars immediately to the sun of Divinity — eagle. (On the arms of a crucifix, these emblems may symbolise humanity, wild and domestic creatures of earth and heaven attending the redeeming sacrifice of their Creator, King and Unifier). e.g. Barton-on-Humber, Lincs. (brass); Bloxham, Oxon. (screen); Dersingham, Norf. (chest); Elkstone, Glos. (door); Halton, Lancs. (churchyard cross); Happisburgh, Suff. (font); Newport, Essex (brass); Shere, Surrey (glass); Stanford-in-the-Vale, Berks.; Surlingham, Norf. (font); Thurcaston, Leics. (brasses).

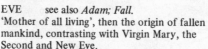

Evangelists' Emblems

EVE   see also *Adam; Fall.*

'Mother of all living', then the origin of fallen mankind, contrasting with Virgin Mary, the Second and New Eve.

> Creation of: Easby, Yorks. (mural); Framlingham, Suff. (tomb); Malvern Priory, Worcs. (glass).
>
> Temptation of: Chaldon, Surrey; Easby,

Yorks. (murals); East Meon, Hants. (font); Norwich cathedral (boss); St. Neot, Cornw. (glass).

EVIL   see also: *Demons; Devil; Sins, Seven Deadly; Virtues and Vices.*

Evil was sometimes represented as a Tree (q.v.) and evil psychology symbolised by a demonic face under a peaked cap e.g. Gresford, Denbighs. (glass); Ludlow, Salop. (stalls); Lydiate Catholic church of Our Lady, Lancs. (alabaster); Peterborough cathedral (boss); Windsor St. George, Berks. (stalls).

EXORCISM

There was an element of exorcism in many rites, especially Baptism, besides a specific service of exorcism involving the use of Holy Water, Holy Oil, Salt, Candles and a Bell, hence 'by bell, book and candle' (the book being the Rituale, containing occasional rites). Exorcist was one of the minor clerical orders along with porter, lector and acolyte.

Exorcism

EXTERIOR IMAGERY   see also *Gargoyles; Sheila-na-gig.*

Apart from the churchyard, images and emblems are found on the external walls of the church, especially above the porch e.g. Monkwearmouth, Durham and on towers e.g. Beauminster, Dorset; St. Austell, Cornw. At Bainton, Yorks., e.g. consecration crosses (q.v.) survive.

FABRIC OF CHURCH

Mediaeval symbolists, such as Durandus, found meaning in walls, windows, vaulting, individual stones and even the mortar binding them together. The symbolic interpretation of church fabric is found in the earliest Christian literature, including the New Testament, though it is usually inverted i.e. the living persons are described in terms of parts of a building.

FABULOUS BEASTS   see also *Evangelists' Emblems.*

Main source in the Bestiary (q.v.)

amphisbaena — winged serpent with second head at tail-tip — deceit and evil.

asp — two-legged beast who laid one ear to

Amphisbaena

Basilisk

Griffin

Manticora

ground and covered other with tail – sinner deaf to divine prompting e.g. Exeter cathedral (misericord).

basilisk – hybrid cock-snake which could kill by its glance – Devil or Anti-Christ e.g. Malvern, Worcs. (misericord); Sheringham, Norf.; Stonham Aspall, Stowlangtoft, Tostock, Suff. (bench-ends); Worcester cathedral (misericord).

blemya – humanoid monster with face in belly – evil, corruption e.g. Norwich, Ripon, Worcester cathedrals (misericords).

caladrius – white bird capable of absorbing human sickness – Christ e.g. Alne, Yorks. (door).

centaur – hydrid man-horse – triumph of animal passions, man torn between spirituality and bestiality, Christ the Avenger or Harrower of Hell, e.g. Adel, Yorks. (capital); Ault Hucknall, Derbys. (tympanum); Beverley Minster, Beverley St. Mary, Yorks. (bosses); Bristol cathedral (boss); Exeter cathedral (boss); Gloucester cathedral (boss); Iffley, Oxon. (capital); Lincoln cathedral (boss); Lullington, Som. (capital); Peterborough cathedral (boss); Westminster abbey (boss); West Rounton, Yorks. (font).

cockatrice – see basilisk.

dragon – reptile-like creature with four legs, wings and tail (barbed) – most frequent symbol of evil e.g. Ault Hucknall, Derbys.

griffin – eagle-lion hybrid – like centaur, an ambivalent symbol: Christ; persecution, covetousness e.g Beverley St. Mary, Yorks.; Cartmel, Lancs.; Charney Bassett, Berks.; Edington, Wilts.; Faversham, Kent.

hydrus – small snake which destroys crocodiles – Christ e.g. Kilpeck, Herefs.

manticora – tri-dentate human head, lion's body, scorpion's tail – evil, destruction e.g. North Cerney, Glos.(graffito).

mermaid – see individual entry.

phoenix – bird renewed from flames – Christ with special reference to resurrection e.g. Queen Camel, Som. (boss); Westminster Henry VII chapel (misericord).

salamander – reptile-like creature who lives unharmed in and on fire – man unscathed by evil and temptation; deadly poison of evil e.g. Salehurst, Sussex; Youlgreave, Derbys. (fonts).

Centaur

Unicorn

sciapod — anthropoid with single monstrous foot under which he can rest in shade — marvel rather than symbol e.g. Dennington, Suff. (bench-end).

siren — two types, classical bird-siren e.g. misericords at Exeter, Lincoln cathedrals, Oxford New College and the more common mermaid (q.v.). Those on misericords at Carlisle cathedral, Hereford All Saints seem a composite of both types — allure, temptation.

Terrobuli — male and female stones which burst into flames when brought together — perils of lust. Very rare examples: Alne, Yorks.; Dalmeny, W. Lothian).

Unicorn — deer-like animal with single horn which could only be captured by a virgin — allegory of the Incarnation. It fights the dragon in castle chapel, Durham. Examples on misericords: Beverley, Yorks.; Boston, Lincs.; Cartmel, Lancs.; Chester, Lincoln cathedrals. Elsewhere: Cambridge, King's College (glass); Clapton, Northants (coffin); Norton, Suff. (font).

Woodwose — see Wild Man (individual entry).

Wyvern — similar to dragon but distinguished by two legs. — heraldic rather than symbolic e.g. Beverley minster, Yorks.: Canterbury cathedral crypt; Newenden, Kent; Weston-in-Gordano, Som.

FALL   see also *Adam, Eve.*

Instinctive symbol resulting from primal fear, insecurity and death. Applied to original sin of archetypal human beings. Their temptation is portrayed on bosses e.g. Beverley St. Mary, Yorks.; Bury St. Edmunds St. Mary, Suff.; their expulsion from Paradise e.g. Ripon, Yorks. and consequent condemnation to toil e.g. Winchester. Temptation and expulsion e.g. Easby, Yorks (mural).

FAST

Voluntary self-discipline by reduction of food, symbolising psychosomatic order against lack of degree. Fasting means limiting quantity, abstinence means doing without (meat). Besides Lent, mediaeval church kept two other long corporate fasts: Advent ('St. Martin's fast') and 'St. John's fast' which ended on June 24th.

FEAST

Liturgical festival celebrated with food, drink and special services. As fasting symbolises self-discipline and sorrow at personal and corporate failings so feasting signifies joy at the spiritual success of others.

'We solemnise the Passion of Christ with a severe fast, but we celebrate the passion of saints with gladness and indulge ourselves somewhat in meat and drink because Our Lord's Passion is a source of shame to us because of our sins. The saints, on the other hand, died not for our sins, but suffered for Christ' (Durandus). Festivals are to strengthen faith, motivate behaviour and sanctify time and are classified as follows:

1. Sundays: feast of re-creation, weekly commemoration of Resurrection.
2. Movable (lunar): Easter, annual commemoration of Resurrection; Pentecost (Whitsunday), annual commemoration of Descent of Spirit. These date from the beginning of the Church and replace the Jewish festivals of Passover and Weeks.
3. Immovable: the commemoration of martyrs or other saints on a fixed date, usually the anniversary of their death. This practice dates before C3 and later certain fixed feasts of Christ (Christmas, Epiphany) and of the Virgin Mary were introduced.

Easter

Canon Law requires attendance at mass and abstention from servile work on major feasts (Holy Day = holiday). Their number was much reduced with the spread of industrial capitalism after the Middle Ages and liturgical holidays are currently a mere eight: Jan. 1st., Jan 6th., Ascension Day, Corpus Christi, June 29, Aug. 15, Nov. 1, Dec. 25th.

FEAST OF FOOLS

Part of Christmas festivities, probably derived from Roman saturnalia but converted to symbolise the paradox of the Incarnation. On or about Jan. 1st. the lowliest minister took charge of the church and its services, even preaching. He was given his wand of office at the appropriate words of the Magnificant (Luke 1.52). This symbolic jollity developed into buffoonery and extravagance and even blasphemy when services were parodied and clergy adopted animal masks (St. David's cathedral, misericord). It was suppressed in 1435. The secular equivalent to the 'Boy Bishop' was the 'Lord of Misrule'.

FEET
The feet of God, Christ and the apostles are always bare in mediaeval iconography — symbolic reference to Isaiah 52.7 cited Rom. 10.15.

FEMALE DEMONS
Horrific figures with breasts do occur, though rarely, e.g. North wall of nave, Canterbury cathedral; nave boss, Winchester cathedral.

FERTILITY SYMBOLS   see *Foliate Head; Jack o'the Green; Paschal Candle; Sheila-na-Gig.*

FETTERS, CHAINS, MANACLES
Attribute of St. Leonard, St. Ninian. Feast of St. Peter's Chains refers to dedication of Roman church with these relics.

Fish

FISH
Most ancient emblem of Christ, derived from acronym of Greek for 'Jesus Christ, Son of God, Saviour'. Very rare occurrence in mediaeval symbolism e.g. St. Just-in-Roseland, Cornw. (boss); Stanground, Hunts. (bench-end); Other fish may be symbolic or heraldic e.g. bosses: Beaulieu, Hants.; Beverley St. Mary, Yorks.; Lacock abbey, Lacock church, Wilts.; St. Madron, Cornw.; or genre e.g. Ockham, Surrey (boss).

Of specific fish, the dolphin is most frequently represented — symbol of Christ, of Resurrection, or of Christian soul e.g. Beverley minster, Yorks.; Ludlow, Salop. (misericords); Piddinghoe, Sussex (weather-vane).

Fish swim in life-giving water surrounding the base of the cross e.g. Taplow, Bucks. (brass) with a double reference as deceased was a fishmonger, and two fish are carved inside the font basin at Bisley, Glos.

Cockles are the badge of St. James and of pilgrims to his shrine and others.

Molluscs occur on bosses e.g. Bury St. Edmund's St. Mary, Suff.; Lacock, Wilts.

Eel seems to symbolise the impediment of evil and occurs on murals of St. Christopher (q.v.)

The crab, with its sideways movement, represents the worldly.

Whale (Aspido Chelone) was legendarily mistaken for an island, destroying sailors so deceived, hence it symbolises the deceits of the Devil e.g. Alne, Yorks.; Bishops Stortford, Herts.; Queen Camel, Som. Its mouth provided an image of Hell-Gate and, with Jonah, it symbolises the Resurrection (see Type) e.g. Ripon, Yorks.

FIVE WOUNDS   see also *Instruments of the Passion; Passion Emblems.*
The wounds of Christ's crucifixion in hands, feet, side symbolise the triumph of His sacrificial love. Popular devotion in later Middle Ages when spirituality centred on the suffering humanity of the incarnate God. (See Wounds) e.g. Broadhembury, Devon (boss); Cambridge Kings College (brass); Dunstable, Beds. (screen).

Five Sacred Wounds

FLOWERS, PLANTS, TREES   see also *Tree.*
almond – divine approval (Numbers 17.1-8). See individual entry.

apple – since 'malum' in Latin could mean 'apple' or 'evil', the apple was identified as the unnamed fruit in Temptation story (Gen. 3). Three apples can be an attribute of St. Dorothy.

aspen – evil. Legend that cross was made from aspen, hence its horrified shivering.

bramble – Blessed Virgin Mary. Traditionally the bush that burned without being consumed (Exodus 3.2) was the bramble.

carnation – pure love (red).

cedar – Christ.

cherry – 'fruit of Paradise'.

clover – Holy Trinity. Shamrock traditionally used by St. Patrick to symbolise this mystery.

columbine – Holy Spirit. Usually portrayed with seven bloom to signify His seven Gifts (q.v.)

fig tree – sometimes identified with the Tree of Knowledge (Gen. 3.7;2.17).

gourd – cucumber. Attribute of St. James the Great, St. Raphael.

grape – communion wine, Blood of Christ, Christ.

Fleur-de-lys

Oak leaves

Rose

hyssop – penance, humility, absolution, baptism (Ps. 51.7)

ilex – holly. Suffering especially Christ's Passion, Crown of thorns.

iris – emblem of Virgin Mary.

laurel – spiritual victory, eternal life.

lily – pre-eminently emblem of Blessed Virgin Mary but also general attribute of virgins. Its heraldic form is the 'fleur-de-lys'.

oak – a sacred tree before arrival of Christianity, as was mistletoe. According to some traditions the cross was made of oak and therefore this wood was a protection against evil. Mistletoe became a symbol of life and love, drawing its substance from the winter oak.

olive – peace. Its oil was the oil of unction, of blessing and consecration.

palm – victory, martyr's triumph over death. See Palm Sunday.

pomegranate – the Catholic Church, e.g. Buckland, Glos. (cope); Newenden, Kent. (font).

reed – supported sponge at Crucifixion (Matt. 27.48). See Instruments of Passion.

rose – most commonly found flower, may be symbolic or naturalistic. Red rose symbolises martyrdom, a white one purity. In general it symbolises triumphant spiritual love: rose wreaths are worn by angels, saints and redeemed souls. Rose associations are complex including the Rose Garden, the Mystic Rose of heaven, the rose without a thorn (Virgin Mary), the chaplet of roses (rosary). The rose can also symbolise Christ's Passion, heaven, or the brevity of earthly life. Attribute of Elizabeth of Hungary and, with apples, of Dorothy.

thorn – crown of, see Instruments of Passion. Parody of festal crown of Romans. Western clerical tonsure reminds clergy that they are servants of One crowned with thorns.

tree – generally a symbol of life but see Tree; Jesse Tree.

wheat – Eucharistic Bread, Christ (John 6.)

vine – extremely common. Symbol of Christ (John 15.1); of wine, especially Eucharistic wine, of Christ's Blood, of life. Mediaeval lore said that the vine repelled toads (evil) and corruption.

Flowers and trees in general symbolise the fruit of good works springing from the root of virtue. They are thus fitting votive offerings to decorate

Foliage

a church, shrine or procession. They also may signify the goodness of natural creation: spring, fertility and rebirth, and formerly wreaths and garlands were hung on church-towers, wells and other sacred objects. Castleton, Derbys. still celebrates Garland Day on May 29th. and well-dressing is still customary in that county. For mediaeval flower processions see Rogation. The ancient goddess of Spring was called Eostre and has left her name in the Christian festival which elsewhere is cognate with Passover.

FOLIAGE

Foliage

Natural and conventional foliage is a dominant decorative feature of mediaeval architecture at all periods. It symbolises life and the goodness of the created order. Conventional foliage often has a trefoil shape referring to the Trinity but many natural leaves become recognisable c. 1250 and flourish in the following century. Creatures often hide in the foliage including Jack o' the Green (q.v.).

FOLIATE HEADS   see also *Jack o'the Green*

Human or animal heads so involved in vegetation as to appear partly or wholly composed of it. The foliage is often oak, sacred to Druids and much revered by Celts. These heads, found on capitals, bosses and misericords, may represent a pagan survival.

FONT

Free-standing baptismal basin, placed near entrance of church for symbolic reasons (see Baptism). From the earliest times fonts and baptisteries were octagonal: eight is symbolical of regeneration, the new creation, as seven is associated with the old. A circular form may be taken as symbolising completion while a chalice-shape associates the two Great Sacraments with complex ramifications (e.g. I John 5.6,8). The decoration of fonts is a rich source of symbolism which extends from God, through Christ and the saints to the mysteries of the Christian faith, virtue and vices to the labours of the agricultural year. Cross saltire is a frequent ornament on Norman fonts. It is significant that X signifies 'a gift' in Runic characters and was also a protection against the poisoned cup i.e. nullified evil within? Particularly

Norman font

notable are the 'Seven Sacrament' fonts common in East Anglia (e.g. Great Witchingham, Little Walsingham, West Lynn). Any selection is invidious but e.g. Ashover, Derbys.; Astwood, Bucks.; Brookland, Kent; Burnham Deepdale, Norf.; Cambridge St. Peter; Castle Frome, Herefs.; Chester cathedral; Colomb Major, Cornw.; Cottam, Yorks.; Dearham, Cumb.; East Meon, Hants.; Elmley Castle, Worcs.; Fishlake, Yorks.; Hook Norton, Oxon.; Horsley Derbys.; Hull Holy Trinity, Yorks.; Huttoft, Lincs.; Ipswich St. Peter, Suff.; Langtree, Devon; Longton, Essex; Minehead, Som.; North Grimston, Yorks.; Offley, Herts.; Orchardleigh, Som.; Pimperne, Dorset.; Stanground, Hunts.; Stanton Fitzwarren, Wilts.; Thornbury, Glos.; Thorpe Salvin, Yorks.; Winchester cathedral; Winster, Derbys.; Winston, Durham.

FONT COVER
Baptismal water was consecrated by a special and complex ritual involving holy oil and blessed salt, consequently there was danger of its being used for superstitious practices. For this, and for hygenic reasons (the font was blessed only twice yearly), it was necessary to protect the water by a lockable cover. At first, this was a closely fitting flat board with metal bands and hasps. Sometimes the side of the font shows damage where hasps were wrenched away at the Reformation. In C14 more complex forms of cover developed; 'tryptich' which was fixed over font and opened like a cupboard e.g. Sedlescombe, Sussex and 'spire' which was raised vertically by pulley and counterweight e.g. Ewelme, Oxon.; Frieston, Lincs.; Halifax, Yorks.; Ufford, Suff.

FONT INSCRIPTIONS
Mediaeval examples at Bradley, Lincs.; Bridekirk, Cumb.; Chelmorton, Derbys.; Dunsby, Lincs.; Potterne, Wilts.; Stafford St. Mary, Staffs.; Terrington St. Clement, Norf.

Post-mediaeval: Dedham, Essex; Knapton, Norf.; Melverley, Salop.; Nottingham St. Mary; Sandbach, Chesh.; Tollesbury, Essex (popular Greek palindrome).

FONT PROJECTIONS
Some mediaeval fonts have projections which

Font cover

Font projection

Font with
symbolic
carving

provided either a shelf to support accessories of
ritual or a drain for disposal of used water e.g.
Odiham, Hants.; Pitsford, Raunds, Northants.

FONT SYMBOLISM

Includes the following subjects:

Adam and Eve: e.g. Bridekirk, Cumb.; East
  Meon, Hants.

Alphabet e.g. Rushton All Saints, Northants.;
  Severnstoke, Worcs.

Angels e.g. St. Merryn, Cornw. (usually with
  shields which were originally filled)

Apostles e.g. Avington, Berks.; Eardisley, Herefs.;
  West Haddon, Northants.

Baptism of Christ e.g. Brighton, Sussex; Castle
  Frome, Herefs.; Portchester, Hants.

Baptism of children e.g. Darenth, Kent; Thorpe
  Salvin, Yorks.

Christ — Agnus Dei, e.g. Bradford Abbas, Dorset;
  Langtree, Devon.
    Crucifixion e.g. Coleshill, Warks.; Lenton,
    Notts.; Lostwithiel, Cornw.
    Other events: Finsham, Norf.; Grantham,
    Lincs.; Kirby, Lancs.

Church e.g. Stanton Fitzwarren, Wilts.

Doctors e.g. Minehead, Som.

Dragons e.g. Chaddesley Corbett, Elmley Castle,
  Worcs.; Winston, Durham.

Evangelists e.g. Aylsham, Great Denham,
  Salthouse, Norf.; Southampton St. Michael,
  Hants.
    Heraldry — usually related to donor e.g. Bolton-
    juxta-Bowland, Yorks.

Lions e.g. Holt, Worcs.; Lostwithiel, Cornw.

Michael e.g. Thorpe Arnold, Leics.

Monograms e.g. Altham, Lancs.; Canterbury
  St. Mildred, Kent; Chipping, Padiham,
  Lancs.

Monsters e.g. Barrowby, Lincs.; Mellor, Derbys.;
  Stone, Bucks.; Thornton Curtis, Lincs.

Months and their Labours e.g. Brookland, Kent;
  Burnham Deepdale, Norf.; Stixwold, Lincs.

Passion e.g. Blakeney, Norf.; Colne, Lancs.; North
  Bradley, Wilts.

Saints e.g. Bakewell, Derbys.; Huttoft, Lincs.;
  Stoke Golding, Leics.

Seasons e.g. Thorpe Salvin, Yorks.

Seven Sacraments e.g. Badingham, Suff.;
  Gresham, Norf.; Melton, Suff.; Sloley, Norf.

Trinity — commonly symbolised by a trefoil
(3 tulips on C17 font, Orston, Notts.)
unusual example at Huttoft, Lincs.

Virgin Mary e.g. Huttoft, Lincs.; Leckhampstead,
Bucks,; Orchardleigh, Som.

Virtues and Vices e.g. Southrop, Glos.; Stanton
Fitzwarren, Wilts.

Woodwose (frequently alternates with lion in
East Anglia) — symbol of unregenerate v.
Christ-like nature (cf. Coloss. 3.9ff).

Zodiac e.g. Brookland, Kent; Hook Norton,
Oxon.

Human heads are extremely common. There
are also grotesques, what appear to be 'genre'
pictures e.g. Belton, Lincs.; Lostwithiel, Cornw.
and images whose meaning is completely lost
e.g. Aston, Yorks.

Foot support

FOOT SUPPORTS

of Effigies in stone or brass. Knights' feet rest on
lions or hounds (courage), their ladies' on dogs
(fidelity). Less common supports have heraldic
reference: bear of Beauchamps, unicorn of
Chaucers, whelk-shell of Willoughbys, elephant
and castle of Beaumonts. Some refer to Christian
name/patron saints of deceased e.g. dragon of
St. Margaret on Margaret Willoughby's brass,
Raveningham, Norf. Others have trade reference:
sheep, wool-pack wine-cask; or are merely
decorative.

FOUR BEASTS   see also *Evangelists'*
Emblems.

Man, lion, ox and eagle (often winged) appear
originally to have referred to four elements of
air, fire, earth and water. Hence, on arms of cross,
they may symbolise the redemption and renewal
of the total creation through the atoning sacrifice
of the God-man (cf. Rev. 21.1,5).

FOURTEEN HOLY HELPERS

Auxiliary Saints. A combination of saints who
became popular around the time of the Black
Death and who were venerated for the supposed
efficacy of their prayers on behalf of a wide
range of human necessities: George, Blaise,
Erasmus, Pantaleon, Vitus, Christopher, Denis,
Cyriacus, Acacius, Eustace, Giles, Margaret,
Barbara, Catharine.

Frid stool

FRID (FRITH) STOOL   see also *Chair*.
'Stool of Peace'. Stone seat (apparently originally bishop's chair) in which sanctuary (q.v.) could be gained if fugitive seated himself in it e.g. Beverley minster, Yorks.; Chewton Mendip, Som.; Ripon cathedral, Sprotborough, Yorks.

FRONTAL   see *Altar Furniture*.

FUNERAL FURNITURE   see *Coffin; Hatchment; Hearse*.

GABRIEL, ST.   see also *Angel*.
Most frequently represented in Annunciation (q.v.) scenes, but does appear on his own e.g. Bradninch, Devon (screen).

GAMBLING
Much condemned in Middle Ages because of its associations: cupidity, profane swearing, wrath (see Sins Seven Deadly; Words.) e.g. Broughton, Bucks. (mural); Norwich cathedral (nave boss); Norwich St. Peter Mancroft (glass). Also associated with Crucifixion (Matt. 27.35) and symbolic dice included among Instruments of Passion (q.v.).

Dice

GAMES, SPORTS, ENTERTAINMENTS
Included in the totality of human life depicted in mediaeval imagery. The world of 'show business' is there with its minstrels, jugglers, contortionists and charlatans. So are the knightly activities of joust, tournament and quest (often with moral implications) and hunting occurs frequently with overtones of the hounds of God and the devil as a roaring lion. There is also a wide selection of popular recreations. e.g. arsey-versey (Ely, Cambs. misericord); backgammon (Manchester, Lancs.: Windsor, Berks. misericords); bear-baiting (Beverley, Yorks.; Enville, Staffs.; Gloucester misericords); other bear activities (Beverley; Boston, Lincs. misericords); blind man's buff (Bristol misericord) 'cock-fighting' (Westminster misericords); contortionists (Ely; Hereford All Saints misericords); dancer (Chichester misericord); face-pulling (Beverley; Chichester; Sherborne, Dorset; Stratford, Warks. misericords); fool (Beverley misericord); football (Gloucester misericord);

hawking (Beverley; Chester; Ludlow, Salop.; Wellingborough, Northants.; Winchester; Worcester misericords); minstrel (Chichester misericord) putting weight? (Exeter boss); quintain (Bristol misericord); quoits (Chester misericord); tumblers (Chichester; Christchurch, Hants.; Hemington, Northants.; Oxford Magdalen, All Saints' misericords); wrestling (Beverley St. Mary boss; Ely misericord; Exeter boss; Halsall, Lancs. Lechlade, Glos.; Leintwardine, Herefs.; Lincoln misericords).

GARDEN

Very complex symbol: place of love, peace and rest. 'Paradise' means 'garden' and there is an earthly and heavenly Paradise. Christ (and the Cross) is the Tree of Life in the midst of the Garden which is irrigated by the 'living water' of the Holy Spirit (also reference to Baptism). God does the planting in His Garden (Matt. 15.13), 'neophyte' means 'newly-planted'. Christ appearing to Magdalen as a Gardener is a common image associating the above ideas with love, restoration (Resurrection).

GARGOYLES AND GROTESQUES

Gargoyle

Gargoyle is a projecting spout to throw water clear of walls, often carved into grotesque or distorted forms so that water comes from a bodily orifice. Corbels are also carved into satyrical or grotesque shapes e.g. Kilpeck, Herefs.; Romsey, Hants. These creations seem more than a play of fancy and probably symbolise demon-haunted air and world of flesh and devil in contrast with the church's realm of salvation and peace. A noteworthy series of grotesques on the bosses of Beverley St. Mary, Yorks., symbolising vices and deadly sins, raises the question whether all grotesques are not representations of evil, sin and vice.

Grotesque

GARLAND, MAIDEN'S   see also *Flowers.*

In C17 and later, when a young woman died unmarried a garland (of real or imitation flowers), often with her collar, glove or kerchief attached, was carried at the funeral and afterwards suspended over her former pew e.g. Abbots Ann, Hants.; Ashford, Derbys.; Astlay Abbots, Salop.; Ilam, Staff.; Minsterley, Salop.

GATE, MAN CARRYING
Samson who is a type (q.v.) of Christ and
symbolises Harrowing of Hell (q.v.) e.g. Norwich
(nave boss); Ripon (misericord); Tattershall,
Lincs. (glass).

Geometrical figures

GEOMETRICAL FIGURES
Equilateral triangle symbolises Trinity (q.v.).
Overlapping of two such triangles produces
Pentalpha (Solomon's seal), of great repute
among exorcists and magicians. Pentagram is a
refuge from evil. Circle is symbol of eternity or
completion (see Ring); three interlaced, of
Trinity. Square represents order, strength,
completion (Rev. 21.16) and may also symbolise
four gospels. Square and Compasses (q.v.) occur
as attributes of God and saints (Jude, Matthew,
Thomas) and on tombs as trade-marks of masons.

GIANTS   see also *Monsters*.
Apart from size, salient characteristic seems to
have been insatiable appetite, consequently
portrayed as devouring animals, humans, or other
monsters. Grotesques with distended mouths
may represent giants. e.g. Sharrington, Norf.
(corbel). The Devil is sometimes conceived as a
devouring giant and occurs in this form in some
Dooms (q.v.) and depictions of the final fate of
Judas. e.g. Amesbury, Wilts.; Cerne Abbas, Dorset
(sculpture); Sherborne, Dorset (misericord);
Winchester cathedral (boss).

GLASS   see also *Stained Glass*.
Windows not only served didactic purposes but
expressed a mystical concept of light. Early
glass often only bore geometrical designs but
later complete theological schemes were
projected through glass: Old Testament types,
New Testament fulfilment, the life and teaching
of Christ, sacraments and doctrines of the
Church, representations of the saints and their
miracles, moral virtues, and the consummation of
all things at the end of the world e.g. Fairford,
Glos.; Malvern, Worcs.; Wintringham, Wragby,
Yorks.; York minster and mediaeval churches.

Glass

GOAT
An ambivalent symbol (see Animals). A boss at
Exeter depicts a man, naked except for a hunting-

71

net, riding a goat and looking back over his shoulder ('Devil rides out' or unknown satire?).

GOD   see also *Christ; Creation; Holy Spirit; Trinity.*
Not represented figuratively before C13. By C16 often vested in papal robes and tiara (q.v.). Earlier, He was symbolised by Hand issuing from cloud (Manus Dei, q.v.). e.g. Clavering, Essex (glass).

GOOSE   see also *Animals.*
'Shoeing the goose' – crass stupidity e.g. Beverley, Yorks.; Whalley, Lancs. (misericord) Geese listening to fox preaching – credulity.

GOSPEL DESK   see also *Lectern.*
Stone book rest on north side of chancel for reading of Gospel at Mass e.g. Crich, Derbys. Combined desk, aumbry and possible Easter sepulchre (q.v.) at Twywell, Northants.

Gospel desk

GRAFFITI
Scratches varying from vandalism to mason's marks (q.v.) and mysterious signs which may indicate fulfilment of a vow (see Votive) e.g. Ford, Sussex; Leighton Buzzard, Beds.; Westham, Sussex. Ashwell, Herts. has a possible drawing of old St. Paul's while Compton, Surrey has a scratch figure of a Norman soldier.

GRAPES, MEN CARRYING
Represent the spies returning from Canaan (Numbers 13.17-27) and typify the rewards of the promised land of heaven gained for His followers by Christ through the shedding of His blood on Calvary. e.g. Ripon, Yorks. (misericord); Twycross, Leics. (glass).

GREEN MAN   see *Jack o'the Green.*

Graffiti

GUILDS, CRAFT AND SOCIAL
Characteristic mediaeval institution, achieving great importance in C14: building chapels, chantries, halls and offering educational, welfare and other social services in addition to their direct concerns. They had a special interest in drama and this, together with their particular patrons and devotions, has left a mark

on iconography e.g. the Mercers' Guild was
devoted to the Assumption which was reflected
in Antingham, Norf. (brass); Coventry Holy
Trinity (misericord); Hinxworth, Herts. (brass);
Stonesfield, Oxon. (glass).

GROTESQUE

Monstrously ugly carved decoration which does
not fit specific or recognisable iconographic
pattern. Grotesques may represent demoted old
gods (like elves and hobgoblins) or the sculptor's
morbid imagination but generally they seem to
be images of evil with protruding tongues (back-
biting, mockery, pains of the damned), hair
standing on end (demoniacal possession). The
problematical 'tooth-ache' faces may actually be
vomiting (gluttony). Some have been interpreted
as indicating the spiritual and physical
deformity wrought by sin and evil in a fallen
world.

Grotesque

HAGODAY   see *Door Knocker; Sanctuary*.
Sanctuary door-knocker, often portraying lion's
head.

HAGIOSCOPE   see *Squint*.

HALO   see also *Vesica Piscis*.
Halo or nimbus is a 'glory' surrounding the
head while the aureole envelops the entire person.
Originally it symbolised power rather than
sanctity. The aureole appeared later and
disappeared earlier than the halo — it signifies
Divine Power as manifested in Assumption,
Doom, Transfiguration e.g. Pedmore, Worcs.
(tympanum); Sandford, Oxon.; Tideswell,
Derbys. (sculpture); Wirksworth, Derbys.
(tomb-cover).

Halo

Christ's halo always has a superimposed
cross; allegorical figures may be haloed, also the
Dove of the Holy Spirit. An evil nimbus occurs
at Idsworth, Hants. (mural). The halo is normally
round but a triangular form sometimes occurs on
representations of God the Father and a square
one on living saints.

HAND   see also *Manus Dei*.
A hand open and uplifted signifies blessing — the
gesture seems to have come from Roman oratory

Hands

but was Christianised by the use of three fingers to symbolise the Trinity. A hand closed over straws refers to the choice between Christ and Barabbas; receiving or holding money, betrayal. Two hands clasped symbolises union and fidelity (the priest binds them together with his stole in the marriage ceremony). Right hand signifies honour. A pair of hands with palms together is a symbol of prayer though the earlier symbol was uplifted arms with palms facing outward.

HARP
Symbol of music (q.v.) and especially of harmony and order. The harp held by David (q.v.) symbolised the Crucifixion — Christ was stretched out like its strings so that he could recreate the original harmony to replace the dissonance of the Fall e.g. York St. Michael Spurriergate (glass).

HARROWING OF HELL
It was a mediaeval tradition that, between His Death and Resurrection, Christ visited the abode of the departed (I Pet. 3.18f). preached there and then led forth the responsive souls, thus giving a retrospective effect to His sacrifice. This attractive doctrine is frequently represented e.g. Ashmansworth, Hants. (mural); East Barming, Kent (bench-end); Lincoln West front (sculpture); Quenington, Glos. (tympanum). The same doctrine is symbolised in Samson's breaking the lion's jaws e.g. Barfreston, Kent (door); Bristol cathedral (misericord); East Barming, Kent (bench-end); Highworth, Wilts. (tympanum); Paington, Devon (chantry carving); Pickering, Yorks.; Stretton Sugwas, Herefs. (tympanum) and in his carrying away the gates (q.v.) of Gaza (though the emphasis here is more on His Resurrection) e.g. Malmesbury, Wilts. (door); Paignton, Devon (chantry); Ripon, Yorks. (misericord); Norwich cathedral (nave boss).

Harrowing of Hell

HART   see *Animals*.

HEAD
On a platter, refers to John the Baptist's decapitation; saint carrying another's head — St. Cuthbert; carrying own head: male — Denis, female — Sitha (Osyth). For heads with

Head carried

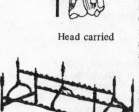

Hearse

protruding tongues, see Grotesques and for heads enmeshed in foliage, Jack o'the Green. Beasts's heads, crowned and mitred, are satirical. Two heads sharing the same features (Janiform) symbolise the Two Natures of Christ while three are a symbol of the Trinity (though some conjoined heads may arise from the exigencies of design). Heads with protruding tongues have been interpreted as phallic symbols or as expressing disrespect, mockery, sacrilege. Heads which glare and menace symbolise demonic forces and biting heads, the destructive aspect of evil. The frequency of heads in mediaeval sculpture has been seen as the effect of pre-Christian head-cult. In general the head is the mirror of personality, the seat of life and reason and symbolises rule, order and control, rational and spiritual man in the image of God.

HEARSE
Iron framework over tomb-effigy to support black pall during Requiem and other funeral services e.g. Warwick; Westminster; West Tanfield, Yorks. Mediaeval palls survive at Arundel, Sussex; Dunstable, Beds.; Norwich St. Gregory.

HEART
Symbol of love and piety (cf. I Sam. 16.7). Sacred Heart with flames and thorns, sometimes surmounted by a cross, emblem of the sacrificial love of Christ e.g. Deane, Hants. (reredos); York minster (West window tracery). Heart pierced by arrow — emblem of Virgin Mary.

HEART BURIAL
Because of their symbolism human hearts were, in extreme circumstances, sometimes given separate burial and indicated by a peculiar memorial ('heart-brass') e.g. Birkin, Yorks.: Brabourne, Kent; Burford, Caversfield, Denton, Oxon.: Fawsley, Northants.; Fordwich, Kent; Leybourne, Kent; Lillingstone Lovell, Bucks.; Margate, Kent; St. Alban's cathedral, Herts.; Wiggenhall St. Mary, Norf.; Yaxley, Hunts.

HEAVEN   see also *Doom;*
Symbolised as the realm beyond the skies, the Eternal City, the Heavenly Garden. The themes

York chapter

St. George

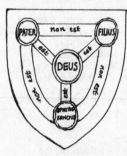

Arms of Trinity

expressed are the victory of goodness and truth, Order and Peace, Joy and Permanence. It is symbolised in the chancel of the church, with its music and white-robed ministers, whose ceiling is often painted blue and bedecked with gold stars. In wall-paintings it is represented as the Kingdom of Christ and the City of God e.g. Pickering, Yorks.

HATCHMENTS
Mourning-board in lozenge-shaped frame giving information about armigerous dead: arms, marital status, etc. It hung for some months before the house of the deceased and was then placed in church e.g. Hoveton St. John, Norf.

HERALDIC MOTIFS   see also *Rebus, Royal Arms.*
Arms of bishops, kings, queens, nobles, abbeys and sees are a rich source of decoration. They sometimes have emblematic significance (see Heraldry, Sacred) but more often refer to patrons and donors, e.g. Lockington, Yorks.; Holt, Denbighs. (font).

HERALDRY, SACRED
The age of chivalry awarded armorial bearings not only to earthly nobility but also to the King of heaven and His citizens (see Arma Virginis, Instruments of the Passion) e.g. Crosthwaite, Cumb.; Darsham, Suff. (fonts).

HERMIT AND ANCHORITE   see also *Vowess.*
Significant element in mediaeval life expressing the desire to be 'Alone with the Alone'. Hermits had their 'holds' by the sea and in fells, fens and forests as well as in towns. They often acted as guides, light-house keepers, bridge and road repairers as well as providing spiritual counsel. Their dress was similar to that of religious orders but distinctive. Anchorites were enclosed in a stricter seclusion and remains of their cells survive in a number of churches e.g. Bengeo, Herts.; Chester-le-Street, Durham; Chipping Ongar, Essex; Compton, Surrey; Hardham, Sussex; Hartlip, Kent; Michaelstow, Cornw.; Newcastle John Baptist, Northd.; Staindrop, Durham; Yateley, Hants.; York All Saints

Anchorage

(reconstruction, lately occupied). There are cave hermitages at Foremark, Derbys.; Kinver, Staffs.; Knaresborough, Yorks.; Roche, Cornw.; Warkworth, Northd.; Wetheral, Cumb. Monuments at Faversham, Kent; Lewes St. John, Sussex; Wellingham, Norf.

HISTORICAL SUBJECTS

The mediaevals regarded the Fall, Flood etc. as historical events if not as trans-historical and therefore contemporary but there are also representations of secular events of national history e.g. on bosses at Bristol, Glos.; Norwich, Norf.; Tewkesbury, Glos.

'HOG BACK'

Viking tomb representing traditional 'house of dead'. Gable-ends have crouching animals and monsters (to ward off evil spirits?) e.g. Appleby, Westm.; Aspatria, Cumb.; Durham cathedral library; Gosforth, Cumb.; Heysham, Lancs.

'Hog back' tomb

HOLY WATER STOUP   see *Stoup*.

HORN

Symbol of puissance, power, virility (as often in Bible). Once paganism was defeated the church tolerated and even encouraged horn rituals and dances (cf. Maypole). Misericord at St. David's cathedral portrays animal mask possibly used in such festivities while Abbot's Bromley, Staffs. keeps horns used in continuing dance.

HORNED WOMAN

Fashionable horned headdress of mediaeval women was much abused by preachers who saw it as a symbol of the devil and of unnatural dominance e.g. 'So the soul which has mastery in a horned woman, as of a butting ox, after reason or the conscience of the preacher shall have warned it that those horns are a cause of damnation to others, is spiritually slain and doomed to everlasting death.' (Bromyard) Undoubtedly a sign of pride e.g. Ludlow, Salop. (misericord). A 'horned man' was a cuckold.

Horned headdress

'HORNY, OLD'

Popular name for Satan. Celtic Europe had worshipped a horned god, often associated with

Horsemen

Hour-glass

a serpent e.g. Kilpeck, Herefs. (door); Lowick, Northd. (frieze).

HORSEMEN
May have apocalyptic reference (Rev. 6) e.g. Norwich (cloister bosses) or represent Magi (q.v.) e.g. Norwich (transept bosses). Mounted saints – either St. George or St. Martin. Questing knights probably have symbolic significance e.g. Beverley St. Mary, Yorks.; Exeter nave, Devon (bosses). A fallen knight probably represents Pride e.g. Norwich (cloister boss) and fighting knights depict the 'Psychomachia' or spiritual conflict e.g. Claverley, Salop. (mural). Some horsemen are merchants (Beverley St. Mary; Selby, Yorks.?) while others may represent the Three Living (q.v.).

HOUR GLASS
Symbol of transitoriness of human life. Actual hour-glasses became a pulpit accessory in C15 and afterwards C16–17 became general e.g. Bloxworth, Dorset; Earl Stonham, Suff.; Hurst, Berks.; Scalby, Yorks.; Tawstock, Devon; Warnham, Suff.

HOURS, CANONICAL
Liturgical prayers (q.v.) which sanctified the day. There were six Day Hours: Prime (first hour) about 6 a.m.; T(i)erce (third hour) about 9 a.m.; Sext (sixth hour) at noon; Nones (ninth hour) about 3 p.m.; Vespers (evening) about 6 p.m.; Compline (night-fall) about 9 p.m. The six day hours were called the Diurnal and were completed by the Night Hours which were divided into three Nocturns (sung in monasteries at midnight, 2 a.m. and 4 a.m.), followed by the dawn service of Lauds. The Nocturns plus Lauds made up Mattins. These prayers were associated with Christ's passion in a popular verse which may roughly be translated:

'At Mattins bound, at Prime reviled, at Terce condemned to death;
Nailed to the Cross at Sext; at None His Blessed Side they pierce.
They take Him down at Vesper-tide; in grave at Compline lay
Who henceforth bids His Church to keep His sevenfold hours alway.'

Censer

Initial letter

HOUSELLING CLOTH
'Housel' means to communicate, to give house-room to Christ in Holy Communion. A linen cloth was attached to communion rails or benches for more reverent reception and to catch any particles of the consecrated Host should they fall. The practice was retained until recently in some churches e.g. Wimborne, Dorset.

INCENSE
Symbol of prayer, especially of adoration (cf. Ps. 151.2; Rev. 8.3f.). Angels carry censers as they mediate between man and God or worship in heaven e.g. Black Bourton, Oxon. (mural); Sall, Norf. (door). Incense also symbolised reverence and dedication, hence persons and objects were liturgically censed: altar, clergy, congregation e.g. bosses at Tewkesbury, Glos.; Westminster, Worcester.

INFANCY
Episodes from the childhood of Christ are represented as symbolising His total identification with humanity e.g. Circumcision at Norwich St. Peter Mancroft (glass); Sall, Norf. (boss); Presentation in the Temple, Elford, Staffs. (glass); Christ with the Doctors, East Harling, Norf.; Malvern, Worcs. (glass). Many events in the life of Christ associated with Virgin Mary are illustrated to show reasons for devotion to her.

INITIAL LETTERS   see also *Monograms.*
A & O – Christ. Alpha and Omega are first and last letters of Greek alphabet, Beginning and End (Rev. 1.8).
BVM – Blessed Virgin Mary (Luke 1.42,45,48)
Chi–rho (q.v.) – Christ.
DNIC – Our Lord Jesus Christ. (Dominus Noster Iesus Christus).
IES – Jesus (first letters – I and J are same in Latin alphabet).
IHS – same as above as capital 'e' is 'H' in Greek but re-interpreted as 'Jesus Saviour of Men' (Jesus Hominum Salvator).

INRI – Jesus of Nazareth, King of the Jews (Latin acronym).

Monograms

IXTHUS – fish. Greek acronym of Jesus Christ, Son of God, Saviour.

M crowned, MR – Maria Regina, Mary Queen of Heaven.

e.g. Blythburgh, Suff. (roof); Congresbury, Som. (boss); East Harling. Norf. (screen); Westminster, St. Stephens cloister (boss).

INNOCENTS, HOLY

Young children massacred by Herod (Matt. 2.1-18) celebrated on Dec. 28th. as representing those who unknowingly die for Christ e.g. Aston, Yorks. (font ?); Chalgrove, Oxon.; Corby, Lincs. (murals); Norwich St. Peter Mancroft; York minster Lady chapel (glass).

INSECTS

Rare and often very unnatural. When they appear they tend to have symbolic significance.

Bee – activity, good order, eloquence, vigilance. Hive is attribute of St. Ambrose and St. Bernard.

Butterfly – Resurrection.

Caterpillar – life e.g. Beverley St. Mary, Yorks.; Exeter cathedral (bosses).

Grasshopper (locust) – can symbolise Christian mission.

Scorpion – evil, treachery, infidelity.

A strange creature, hoofed, crowned and saddled on Exeter cathedral misericord has been identified as the 'locust of the Apocalypse' (Rev. 9.7).

Locust of the Apocalypse

INSTRUMENTS OF THE PASSION

Include Cross, spear, crown of thorns, scourges, reed with sponge, nails, pillar of scourging, dice, seamless raiment, pincers, lantern, Peter's cock, label (INRI superscription), ladder, hammer, vernicle (q.v.) These emblems were indulgenced and provided with prayers against sins and weaknesses so symbolised e.g. 30 pieces of silver and treachery, betrayal, covetousness; lantern and the dark night of sin, deeds of darkness; vinegar & gall and the poison of sin; sponge on reed and gluttony; spitting and the forgiveness of enemies, contemners; entombment and good death. They appear as the armorial bearings of Christ by end of C16 and are borne on shields

Instruments and Emblems of the Passion

Instruments of the
Passion

by angels. They are frequent on roof bosses but may occur almost anywhere e.g. Almondbury, Yorks.; Beeston Regis, Norf.; Braunton, Devon (bench end); Coyty, Glam. (parish chest); Lechlade, Glos. (boss); Kilkhampton, Cornw. (bench-end); Llanrwst, Denbighs. (screen); Newton St. Cyres, Devon (boss); Queen Camel, Som. (boss); Sall, Norf. (porch); Sefton, Lancs. (bench-end); Silkstone, Yorks.; Stogumber, Som. (capital).

IRONWORK
May be wrought into symbolic form e.g. fleur-de-lys. Sometimes strap-work on doors is splayed to form letter 'C' allegedly referring to St. Clement, patron of blacksmiths.

Jack O'the green

JACK O'THE GREEN
Perhaps commonest single motif if we include Foliate Heads (q.v.) which seem of same genre. Probably Celtic in origin but very popular in C14–C15 when it was freely absorbed into Christian iconography. Originally, it seems to refer to the spirit of foliage and vegetable life and is related to the rites of Spring (see Maypole). Later it symbolised the New Life theme of Easter but it may retain some sinister associations of corrupted nature. e.g. Coventry Holy Trinity, Warks. (misericord); Crowcombe, Som. (bench-end); Dorchester, Oxon. (corbel); Dover, Kent (spire); Oxford Christchurch (boss).

JAIRUS' DAUGHTER
Her raising from the dead (Mark 5.22), together with that of Lazarus (John 11.1-44), were the commonest exemplars of 'I am the Life' and their symbolic use dates from the earliest Christian centuries. e.g. Brook, Kent; Copford, Essex; (murals).

'JANGLING'   see also *Tutivillius; Words, Idle.*
Idle or malicious gossip, especially in church. Much inveighed against by preachers since it combines malice, sloth and sacrilege e.g. Colton, Norf.; Peakirk, Northants.; Seething, Norf.; Wiston, Suff. (murals).

Jesse Tree

JESSE, TREE OF

Representation of Christ's human genealogy in conventional form of tree. It is rooted in Jesse, branches bear later ancestors and its crown is the Virgin and Child. The tree sometimes bears pagan prophets including sybils (q.v.) and Vergil. The tree is often a vine (q.v.) and, like the Cross, is a tree of salvation e.g. Abergavenny, Mon. (sculpture); Abingdon St. Helen, Berks. (painting); Black Bourton, Oxon. (mural); Christchurch, Hants. (reredos); Dyserth, Flints. (glass); Dorchester, Oxon. (glass); Elton, Northants, (mural); Lowick, Northants. (glass); Madley, Herefs. (glass); Margaretting, Essex (glass); Merevale, Warks. (glass); Morpeth. Northd. (glass); Thornhill, Yorks. (glass); Selby, Yorks. (glass); Shrewsbury St. Mary, Salop. (glass); Waltham Abbey, Essex (glass); Weston Longville, Norf. (mural).

JOYS OF MARY

The Joyful Mysteries of the Rosary (q.v.) namely: Annunciation, Visitation, Nativity, Presentation, Finding in the Temple (Luke 2.42-50). A common mediaeval prayer was: 'Mary, for thy joyes five, help me live in clene live.'

Judas' kiss

JUDAS   see also *Fish*.

Archetypal symbol of betrayal and treachery, with associations of covetousness. He is usually represented with a money-bag (John 12.6) which symbolises preference for earthly over heavenly treasure. At the Last Supper, he may symbolise sacrilegious communion. Kiss of betrayal e.g. Hawkley, Hants. (alabaster); Launcells, Cornw. (bench-end); Poughill, Cornw. (bench-end). Suicide and final end e.g. bosses at Amesbury, Wilts.; Southwark cathedral, London; Winchester cathedral nave (boss); Wotton-under-Edge, Glos.

JUDGMENT, LAST   see *Doom*.

KALENDAR

Archaic spelling sometimes used to distinguish ecclesiastical Kalendar of Feasts and Fasts, Seasons and Holy Days from the secular calendar of State and Bank Holidays.

KEY

Attribute of St. Peter (Matt. 16.9) associated
with stewardship, binding and loosing in name
of master. Later tradition sometimes distinguished
key for opening heaven from one for locking hell.
Key on coffin slab may indicate butler, steward,
cellarer etc. Key and Pail on tower at Soberton,
Hants. are supposed to refer to butler and
domestic servant involved in its erection.

King

KINGS AND QUEENS

Their heads appear on corbels, pier-heads, drip-
moulds etc. Sometimes they are Anglo-Saxon
saints, otherwise they represent founders,
benefactors, patrons or merely contemporary
rulers. St. Edmund, St. Edward the Confessor
and Henry II appear on bosses at Tewkesbury
and Norwich and the murder of Edward II is
depicted on bosses at Bristol cathedral. Beverley
St. Mary, Yorks. has Athelstan and Wimborne
Minster, Etheldred. David appears in Worcester
cloister boss and the May King in Exeter quire.
Queens are less frequent but occur e.g. at
Overbury, Worcs.; Norwich St. Helen's Hospital.

KNEELERS   see also *Weepers.*

1. Cushions for kneeling.
2. Representations of dependents (often
Bedesmen) praying for the departed on their
monuments e.g., brass: Hildersham, Cambs.
Almshouses, Bedehouses (e.g. Castle Rising,
Norf.) and Hospitals often accommodated such
beneficiaries on condition of praying for
benefactor.

Knight and Lady

KNIGHTS AND LADIES

Portrayed in brass, glass and recumbent effigies.
Crossed legs do not indicate crusader but posture
seems peculiar to England e.g. Auckland, Durham;
Bainton, Yorks.
Brasses: Aldbury, Herts.; Burghwallis, Yorks.;
     Chartham, Kent; Lambeth St. Mary, London;
     Lillingstone Dayrell, Bucks.; Sheppey, Kent;
     Stoke D'Abernon, Surrey; Westley Waterless,
     Cambs.; Wymington, Beds.
Effigies: Bottesford, Leics.; Darrington, Yorks.;
     Dorchester, Oxon; Goodhurst, Kent; Lowick,
     Northants.; West Tanfield, Yorks.
Glass: East Harling, Norf.; Long Melford, Suff.;

Tewkesbury Abbey, Glos.; York minster nave.

The Church tried to reform and civilise the caste-system of knighthood by associating it with consecrating ritual, placing it under the protection of patronal saints and emphasising its obligations to support the church, defend the weak, uphold right and punish evil-doers. These ideas are expressed in representations of St. George which show the emblematic lamb, the helpless princess and the defeated dragon of evil.

KNOCKER   see *Door*.

KNOTS

Originally connected with sympathetic magic and the ideas of binding, making helpless or faithful (of which True Lovers' Knot is a survival). A knot, knob or knop provides the divisions of the Rosary (q.v.). A knot may be heraldic (as in Stafford knot). Knots occur on bosses at Chumleigh, Devon; Lanreath, Cornw.; Ockham, Surrey; Sherborne, Dorset; Windsor St. George, Berks.

Sowing the crop

LABOURS OF THE MONTHS

Representations of typical seasonal work, believed to be result of Fall e.g. Calverton, Notts. The series show regional differences and few complete sets survive e.g. Brookland, Kent (font); Ripple, Worcs. (misericords). Examples of individual labours survive at Beverley St. Mary, Yorks. (boss); Burnham Deepdale, Norf. (font); Carlisle cathedral (capitals); Easby, Yorks. (mural); Gloucester (misericord); Leicester town hall (glass); Lincoln cathedral (cloister boss); Malvern, Worcs. (misericord); St. Albans cathedral, Herts. (watching-loft); Worcester cathedral (misericord); Worle, Som. (misericord).

LABYRINTH

The maze was a pre-Christian symbol of life and may be associated with sun-worship. It was Christianised to symbolise the tortuous path from birth to Paradise: there is only one way which leads to the centre. Mazes may also have been used as substitutes for pilgrimages. Great churches (e.g. Chartres) had them inlaid in the floor, others had turf-mazes in the vicinity e.g. Alkborough, Lincs.; Dalby, Yorks.; Guildford St. Martha, Surrey; Saffron Walden, Essex; Winchester

Maze

cathedral. Mazes appear on bosses at Bristol St. Mary Redcliffe; South Tawton, Devon.

LADY CHAPEL

In churches not dedicated to Virgin Mary, a chapel was added with this dedication (usually in C13 and C14). In greater churches, it was normally built at the East end behind the High Altar. In lesser ones it tends to be in an aisle. This architectural development reflected the developing cult of the Queen of Heaven and the consequent 'feminisation' of Western culture. e.g. Chipping Sodbury, Glos.; Fordham, Cambs.; Grantham St. Wulfram, Lincs.; High Wycombe, Bucks.; Long Melford, Suff.; Patrington, Yorks.

LAITY   see also *Nave.*

The 'laos' (people) of God to whom certain of its duly ordained members minister. The powerful lay element in mediaeval Christianity is shown in the guilds, drama etc. The laity are frequently represented in ecclesiastical imagery which includes not only knights and ladies (q.v.) but blacksmiths and viragos, minstrels and other entertainers, dishonest alewives and saintly women, aristocratic activities and domestic brawls.

LAMP   see also *Candles; Lighting.*

The artificial illumination of mediaeval churches usually came from a single source symbolising Christ the Light of the World. In some places this took the form of an elaborate candelabrum or 'corona lucis' e.g. Bristol Temple Church and modern example at Buckfast Abbey, Devon. Sometimes there were seven lamps about or before the High Altar (Rev. 4.5) and there were seven candles on it when a bishop celebrated Mass. The origins of this may be in the seven-branched candle of the Jewish sanctuary. Devotional lights are a development of the classical oil lamp with a wick floating on olive oil and modern use is to have a white light before Blessed Sacrament, blue before statues of Virgin Mary and red in front of other saints (see Colour).

Lamp

LAST SUPPER   see also *Maundy Thursday.*

Very common image because of its symbolism of

85

communion, Eucharist, love e.g. Ashby St. Ledger, Northants. (mural); Brighton St. Nicholas, Sussex (font); Madley, Herefs. (glass); Malvern, Worcs. (glass); North Grimston, Yorks. (font); Sall, Norf. (boss); Tewkesbury, Glos. (boss).

LECTERN

Lectern

Reading desk or stand, usually of wood or metal and portable, more rarely of stone and fixed (see Gospel Desk). Mediaeval use for support of large music books in choir or for Gospels. Reformed church used them for Bible stands from which the lessons were read at Morning and Evening Prayer and this adaptation has ensured the survival of some mediaeval lecterns. These were sometimes two-sided or even four-sided but the commonest remaining form is single-side on which a bird, usually eagle or pelican (q.v.), supports the book on its out-stretched wings e.g. Lincoln cathedral; Middleton, Hants.; Stanton Fitzwarren, Wilts.; Wells cathedral; York Minster. Unusual birds e.g. cock, Wednesbury, Staffs.; turkey (badge of Stricklands), Boynton, Yorks. Other interesting examples: Astbury, Ches.; Bledlow, Bucks.; Bury, Hunts.; Cavendish, Suff.; Croft, Lincs.; Cropredy, Oxon.; Edenham, Lincs.; East Hendred, Berks.; East Leake, Notts.; Isleham, Cambs.; Laughten-en-le-Morthen, Yorks.; Leighton Buzzard, Beds.; Little Gidding, Hunts.; Long Sutton, Lincs.; Lowestoft, Suff.; Monksilver, Som.; Newcastle, Northd.; Newchurch, Hants.; Norwich cathedral; Ottery St. Mary, Devon; Oundle, Northants.; Phillack, Cornw.; Southwell, Notts.; Wiggenhall St. Mary, Norf.; York All Saints Pavement, Yorks.

LEGENDS OF SAINTS

Much mediaeval imagery is unintelligible without some knowledge of legendary material which was attached even to New Testament characters. This is most easily obtained from one of the many editions of 'The Golden Legend'. e.g. Catherine (mural: Sporle, Norf.)

George (glass: St. Neot, Cornw.; mural: Hardham, Sussex).

Helen (glass: Ashton-u-Lyne, Lancs.; Morley, Derbys.)

James (mural: Guildford St. Mary, Surrey)

John (bosses: Norwich cathedral cloisters;
    Westminster St. Mary's crypt).
Lawrence (alabasters: Lanteglos, Cornw.;
    Ludlow St. Lawrence, Salop.)
Martin (sculpture: Wareham, Dorset).
Mary, Blessed Virgin (murals: Chalgrove, Oxon.;
    Croughton, Northants.)
Matthias and Andrew (glass: Greystoke, Cumb.)
Nicholas (glass: Banwell, Som.; font: Brighton
    St. Nicholas, Sussex; glass: Hillesden, Bucks.;
    Mere, Wilts.; boss; Norwich cathedral; font:
    Winchester cathedral).
Theophilus (reredos: Beverley minster, Yorks.;
    St. Denys Walmgate, Yorks.)

Martyrdom of
St. Edmund

LENT   see also *Shrove Tuesday*.
Principal Christian fast and period of penitence
from Ash Wednesday (q.v.) to Easter Eve in
which Christ's forty days in the wilderness in
commemorated and imitated. The word is
derived from the old English for 'Spring'.
Lenten lily is daffodil.

LENTEN VEILS
'Now all things which pertain to the ornament
of a church must be removed or covered over in
the season of Lent' (Durandus) symbolising
(*a*) the Church's mourning and penitence,
(*b*) Christ's suffering in the flesh with His
    Godhead veiled,
(*c*) the imperfect revelation of God before Christ's
    death and resurrection.
In the Middle Ages a curtain (the so-called
'Hunger-cloth') was dropped before the
sanctuary to veil the altar. The great crucifix
alone was unveiled during the ceremonies of
Good Friday to become the sole object of
devotion.
   'On Holy Saturday all the veils and curtains
are removed because the veil of the temple was
rent during the Passion of our Lord' (Durandus).
   In the middle ages, statues etc. were veiled
in unbleached linen sometimes bearing a red
cross; modern usage is purple stuff and to limit
veiling to Passiontide perhaps in reference to
words in Gospel of Passion Sunday – 'He hid
himself'.

Cresset light

LIGHTING   see also *Candle; Lamp.*
There was little need for general lighting in the mediaeval church. Most services took place in day-light and altar candles and those attached to reading-desks were adequate for the Night Hours. General lighting was provided by a cresset, a stone with one or more hollows which contained oil and floating wicks e.g. Dearham, Cumb.; Lewannick, Cornw.; North Wingfield, Derbys.; Romsey, Hants.; Wareham, Dorset; Weston, Yorks.; Wool, Dorset.

Most lights were devotional or symbolic (see Votive); on altars, before rood, statues and shrines. A candle-sconce survives at Piddinghoe, Sussex; a candle-pricket at Rowlstone, Herefs., and a rushlight holder at Warnham, Sussex.

LILY
Symbol of Virgin Mary conventionalised into 'fleur-de-lys'. In its 'natural' form it is usually given six leaves symbolising holiness and purity of body, purity of heart, meekness, Godly fear, self-discipline, steadfastness. It can also symbolise the body of her Son or carry even more complex meanings (see Lily Crucifix). It is usually in a pot or vase and may be replaced by an iris. The pot itself is significant being either a symbol of Our Lady's virginity or referring to the 'pot of manna' laid up in the tabernacle (Ex. 16,33; Heb.9,4) e.g. Kingswood Abbey Gatehouse Glos.

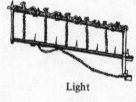

Light

LILY CRUCIFIX
Lily supporting crucifix e.g. Abingdon, Berks. (painting); Tong, Salop, (misericord); York Minster choir (glass). A complex symbol of re-creation, combining allusion to Annunciation (Incarnation) with Crucifixion (Redemption). Traditionally, the two events took place on the same date – March 25th.

'A man is strengthend nobly;
That he no pain may feel,
Of this flower, Christ-on-Cross,
Beholding the colour.'

Mediaeval preachers taught that the flower represented the seven gifts of the Holy Spirit (q.v.), that its touch assuaged pride, its scent induced pity, its fruit calmed anger, its leaves warned against avarice, its juice

Light

Lily

supported the intellect against gluttony, its taste strengthened wisdom against lust and its colour gave fortitude.

LITERARY REFERENCE
Some mediaeval iconography has a literary source, varying from popular tales (e.g. Reynard the Fox) to romances e.g. misericords at Beverley minster, Yorks. and Darlington, Durham (Alexander's flight to the world's end); Chester cathedral (Red Riding Hood); Enville, Staffs. (Sir Yvain); Exeter (Knight of the Swan); Gloucester; Lincoln (Tristram and Iseult).

LITURGICAL PRAYER
Much symbolism is derived from the formal prayer of the Church in accordance with the principle that 'the rule of prayer is the rule of faith'. This prayer is largely Scriptural and therefore makes use of the traditional Biblical exegesis in terms of type (q.v.) and analogy.

   'The principles on which are founded the variations in ecclesiastical offices take the hue of the four senses of Scripture: the historical, allegorical, topological, anagoeical with the gold of faith as the ground.' (Durandus).

LITURGICAL WORSHIP
One of the basic themes of religion is the 'sanctification of time', making all time holy and not just 'mythical time' and also rendering contemporary the events of the 'great time'. Christianity attempts to do this through the Liturgical Year which brings a cyclic renewal of salvation-history and enables the worshipper to participate in it as he proceeds from Advent to Christmas and Epiphany and thence through Lent to Holy Week and Easter and finally to the Ascension and Pentecost, taking in along this course the heavenly birthdays of his predecessors and assistants. Such an approach is of a piece with the central act of Christian worship which re-presents the events of Maundy Thursday and unites them, as apparently Christ did, with the recall of His Death and Resurrection. The liturgy itself is thus pre-eminently a prayed and prayerful symbol.

Lychgate

Lychnoscope

Madonna

LOW SIDE WINDOW   see *Lychnoscope*.

LYCH GATE   see also *Burial*.
Gated and gabled entrance to 'God's acre' where the coffin rested temporalily on a wooden or stone support (see Coffin Stool) for the first part of the burial service. The words mean 'corpse gate' and it symbolises the gate of death and this symbolism is sometimes developed e.g. Hickleton, Yorks. Few lych gates antedate C17 and the earliest ones seem to be at Anstey, Herts.; Beckenham, Boughton, Winchelsea, Kent; Hartfield, Sussex; Kellington, Yorks. A coffin-table survives at Chiddingfold, Surrey.

LYCHNOSCOPE
Small opening usually associated with westernmost window on south side of chancel. Only found in parish churches and often shuttered. Purpose obscure but definitely not a 'Leper window'. Of the dozen or so explanations offered the most likely one seems that it was to allow a minister inside the church to ring a sacring bell (see Bell, sacring) to inform them of the high point of mass e.g. Ardingly, Sussex; Buckland, Kent; Dinder, Som.; Chiddingfold, Surrey; Kemerton, Glos.; Kingston-next-Lewes, Old Shoreham, Sussex; Othery, Som.; Melton Constable, Norf.; Rampton, Cambs.
    There may be a connection between this facility and squints and some pierced screens. Lychnoscopes seem to have been unneccessary when the sacring bell was placed in a bell-cote or provided in the bell tower.

MADONNA   see also *Christ: Virgin Mary*
'My lady', an image of Mary holding the Christ child. Mother and child is a powerful aboriginal symbol of creation, love and sacrifice but its force is infinitely increased when the Son is believed to be God Himself made man for the redemption of the world.

MAGDALEN   see also *Noli me tangere*.
A favourite subject symbolising triumph of grace over pride and the transition through love and repentance from sensuality to contemplation. Represents the restoration of psychological order and harmony. Her

significance is intensified by the fact she is chosen to be the first witness of the Resurection (John 20). In the Middle Ages she was conflated with the repentant woman of Luke 7.36-50), and with Mary of Bethany (John 12) e.g. Combe-in-Teignhead, Devon (bench-end); Little Wenham, Suff. (mural); Wells cathedral (West front); Westminster Henry VIII chapel (sculptures).

MAGI

Wise men from the East (Matthew 2.1-12). The mediaevals made them three in number, gave them the status of kings, and associated specific gifts with each. They even provided them with names and descriptions: aged Caspar with a long grey beard, Melchior in the prime of life and having a short beard, Balthasar young and beardless and sometimes a negro. These three, always taken to represent the Gentiles coming to Christ, were later taken to symbolise the three races of the inhabited world. Their gifts have always been given symbolic significance: gold – Kingship of Christ, faith; incense – Divinity of Christ, prayer; myrrh – Christ the Saviour – suffering and self-discipline. e.g. Bishopsteignton, Devon; Buckland-in-the-Moor, Devon (screen); Christchurch, Hants. (rerdos); Gresford, Denbighs.; Madley, Herefs. (glass); Plymtree, Devon (screen).

Boss: magi

MAGNIFICAT

Song of the Virgin Mary (Lk. 1.46-55) from its first word in Latin. Symbolises the Divine paradox of the world's values being turned upside down and thus right way up – the same ideas are expressed in the Beatitudes (Matthew 5.3-10) and also in the Feast of Fools (q.v.). A Magnificat window survives at Malvern, Worcs.

MAJESTAS

Image of Christ in Majesty come to judge the living and dead (see Doom) in contrast to the silence and humility of His first Advent e.g. Barnack, Northants.; Daglingworth, Glos. The details are derived mainly from Revelation. He is usually seated and robed (but the wounded side may be disclosed), He may wear the Crown of Thorns, and the hands may be raised or

Majestas

support an orb or a book. The accompanying angelic trumpeters distinguish this subject from the similar one of the Triumphant Christ which also has the themes of light, radiance (and often supporting angels). It was a favourite subject over doors (q.v.) e.g. Adel, Yorks.; Elkstone, Glos.; Essendine, Rutland; North Newbald, Yorks.; Prestbury, Ches. and for murals e.g. Copford, Essex; Kempley, Glos.; Newington, Bucks. It is found elsewhere e.g. bosses in cathedrals of Ely, Exeter, Gloucester, Wells, Winchester.

MALCHUS

Malchus' ear

High Priest's servant whose ear was cut off by Peter during Christ's arrest in Garden of Gethsemane (John 18.10). He is often portrayed with a lantern e.g. Drayton, Berks.; Hawkley, Hants. (alabasters). He also appears at East Brent, Som. (glass); East Harling, Norf. (glass); Winchester cathedral (choir boss); Windsor St. George, Berks. (stalls). Malchus' ear can occur among Instruments of Passion (q.v.).

'Peter cut off Malchus's ear and Christ restored it. From this we may see that if a man hear not (the Church), his ear must be spiritually smitten off by Peter; for it is Peter who has the power of binding and loosing' (Mediaeval gloss on Canon Law).

MALLET-GOD

Celtic divinity Succellos, related to fertility and plenty. Attributes: mallet, dog, dish of plenty e.g. Codgrove St. Peter, Wilts.; Copgrove, Yorks.

MANUS DEI

Manus Dei

Hand of God issuing from a cloud, emblem of God the Father who was not represented full-figure before C13. e.g. Black Bourton, Oxon.; Brook, Kent (murals); Clavering, Essex (glass); Castle Frome, Herefs. (font); Cliffe-at-Hoo, Kent (mural); Elkstone, Glos. (sculpture); Hamstall Ridware, Staffs. (paten); Lenton, Notts. (font); Little Missenden, Bucks. (mural); Romsey, Hants. (sculpture).

MARIAN DEDICATIONS   see also
Dedication; Lady Chapel.
Crescendo of Marian piety began in C12 and

dedications to the Mother of Christ take many forms: St. Mary, St. Mary the Virgin, Blessed Virgin, Blessed Virgin Mary, Our Lady, Our Lady of Pity, St. Mary of Charity, St. Mary de Grace, Lady St. Mary, Lady of Sorrows, Mother of God. The multiplication of Marian dedications led to necessary distinctions between churches in the same town: St. Mary the Great, St. Mary the More, St. Mary the Less, St. Mary Junior, St. Mary le Bon, St. Mary alder Mary. There were dedications to Marian 'apparitions' such as Our Lady of Evesham, Walsingham cf. modern Lourdes, Fatima. There are also dedications to Marian 'mysteries' e.g. Annunciation, Purification. Salutation (visitation), Conception, Nativity and (particularly) Assumption.

MARKS   see also *Graffiti*.

It was the practice for a mason to put his peculiar mark on stones he had dressed to identify his work (and perhaps to check his output). Simple marks which are not individual are probably 'position marks' for the guidance of stone setters. The marks on the screen at Norwich St. John Maddermarket may be the identifying marks of craftsmen or donors.

Mason's marks

MARRIAGE SYMBOLS

Veil: modesty, virginity, consecration (ideal – previous virginity and subsequent fidelity, sometimes beyond death – see Vowess).

Wedding ring

Ring: completion, a couple-union. Belief that there was a vein direct from heart (q.v.) to fourth finger, hence ring on this finger signifies union of hearts (couples gave each other a ring).

Hands bound together by priest's stole – plighting of troth before God, binding together for ever.

Rice, grain – pre-Christian fertility symbol, now replaced by even more objectionable confetti.

Catholic tradition disapproves of solemnisation of matrimony (a joyful event) within penitential seasons such as Lent and Rogationtide. Nuptial Mass takes place immediately after wedding (originally at church door) at which fasting couple communicate together in the Body of Christ (hence wedding breakfast).

Christian marriage symbolises the union between Christ and His Church, between the soul and God and between the two natures (human and divine) in Christ. Ancient Christian tradition was unhappy about second marriages even after the death of one partner. Alone among Christian sacraments (q.v.) the ministers are always lay — the couple marry each other, the cleric only acts as a witness and gives the Church's blessing.

Mask

MARY, THE BLESSED VIRGIN   see *Virgin Mary*.

MASKS

Masks symbolise personality. They were used to depict evil characters in miracle plays. Iconography provides bestial or grotesque visages for evil-doers e.g. Little Missenden, Bucks (mural); Norwich St. Peter Mancroft, Norf. (glass); West Chiltington Sussex.

Masks were also worn at the Feast of Fools (change of character?).

Mason's marks

MASONS   see also *Marks*.

Master masons were the builder-architects of the Middle Ages and held high status in that functional society. They are often portrayed with measuring rod, compasses and set-square. These tools are also symbols of order and design, of replacing chaos by structure. Geometry was central to mediaeval academic education and provides the basis for Gothic architecture. Perhaps they were aware of Plato's remark that God was an eternal geometriser (see Compasses). Set square and compasses e.g. Peterborough choir boss.

Communion wafer

MASS

Central act of Christian worship and 'raison d'etre' of all mediaeval and other Catholic churches. It commemorates the Last Supper and is seen as a lively memorial/re-presentation of Christ's sacrifice and the sharing of communicants and others in its benefits and effects. In the Middle Ages its sacrificial aspect was over-emphasised at the expense of other elements, resulting in the multiplication of masses, altars, chantries etc. Mass was offered at least once daily in all parish churches except on Good

Anglo saxon oven
for baking
eucharistic wafer

Friday and parishioners were expected to be present on all Sundays and Holy Days. The wheaten wafers consecrated at this rite are believed to become the Body of Christ (Corpus Christi) and are called Hosts (victims). The consecrated bread (Blessed Sacrament) was kept in church for sick communions and adoration (see Easter Sepulchre, Pyx, Aumbry). Because of their destined use these wafers were usually baked in a convent or church (Saxon oven: Thursley, Surrey).

MASS DIAL   see *Dial*.

Mass of St. Gregory

MASS OF ST. GREGORY
Gregory (540–604) was Pope, initiator of the Roman mission to England, reformer, musician, doctor and patron of Benedictine monasticism. He had a very literal view of Christ's Real Presence in the Mass exemplified in the story of Christ descending from the altar with the Instruments of the Passion (q.v.) to convince a sceptic. He also emphasised the efficacy of Mass offered on behalf of souls in Purgatory. Rare surviving representations e.g. Hillesden, Bucks.; Herstmonceux, Sussex (brasses); Paignton, Devon (alabaster); Stoke Charity, Hants.

Washing of feet

MAUNDY THURSDAY   see also *Last Supper*.
Name derived from opening words of Mass on Thursday in Holy Week: 'Mandatum novum' – 'A new commandment (I give unto you, that ye love one another)'. Christ then exemplified one aspect of this love by washing the feet of His disciples – a ceremony that was imitated by bishops, abbots and others on this day. (Maundy money is a sort of commutation.) It was also celebrated as the day of institution of Mass, Eucharist, Holy Communion. Public penitents were restored to the church on this day after Lenten penance and formal absolution. e.g. Sall, Norf. (boss); Somerton, Oxon. (reredos); Southwell, Notts. (capital); Wirksworth, Derbys. (carving).

MAY DAY
May 1st., the traditional Spring festival, incorporated into Christian rejoicings e.g. Choristers on Magdalen tower, Oxford, processions of white-robed maidens with flowers

Maypole

May King and Queen

Maypole base

Memento mori

and foliage and song and dance, Queen of the
May, Maypole. Hooks for the support of the
maypole sometimes survive in external church
wall and the stone in which its base was set
survives at Shalford, Surrey. Catholics tried to
associate May with Mary. The Puritans abolished
the festivities because of their pagan associations
(as they tried to do with Christmas.) See also
Foliate Heads, Rogationtide.

MAYPOLE
A phallic symbol associated with fertility dance.
Dancing round the maypole was tolerated and
even protected by the mediaeval Church. (See
May Day.) Maypoles at e.g. Aldborough, Yorks.;
Barwick-in-Elmet, Yorks.; Bledington, Glos.;
Ickwell, Beds.; Nun Monkton, Yorks.; Slingsby,
Yorks.

MAZE   see *Labyrinth*.

MEMENTO MORI   see also *Dance of Death*.
Three Living . . .
'Remember that you have to die' – a message
constantly repeated in the ceremonies of Ash
Wednesday (q.v.), passing bell, cadaver tombs
(e.g. Feniton, Devon; Paignton, Devon), death's
heads and skeletons (e.g. Barnington Parva,
Norf. (poppy-head); Biddenham, Beds.; Childrey,
Berks.; Shipton-under-Wychwood, Oxon.
(brasses). The theme became even more popular
in the Jacobean period e.g. Cox monument at
Broxbourne, Herts. which develops the mediaeval
tradition exemplified at Ewelme, Oxon.; Holme,
Notts.; Oxted, Surrey; Sturrey, Kent; Swinbrook,
Oxon. A similar message was often inscribed on
sundials and emblems of mortality multiplied:
hour-glass, inverted torch, scythe, shattered
column, cinerary urn. Lych gate at Hickleton,
Yorks. has two enclosed skulls with the
inscription: 'Today for me; to-morrow for thee.'

MERMAID
Frequent symbolical subject e.g. Bakewell,
Derbys.; Boston, Lincs.; Halifax, Yorks.; Malpas,
Ches.; Stratford, Warks. The mermaid is
conflated with Siren (q.v.) as a seductress and
her half-human form has the common
signification of the dominance of animal nature
e.g. Long Stow, Hunts.; Nately Scures, Hants.

Mermaids

She represents pride (mirror), deceit and luxury or lust. A fish grasped in one hand represents a Christian soul in the grip of diabolical deceit. Mermaid's mirror also represents self-centredness e.g. Exeter (boss); Norwich cathedral; Nantwich, Ches.; Ludlow, Salop. (misericords); Sherborne, Dorset (boss). Complex symbol of mermaid suckling lion at Edlesborough, Bucks.

The merman is the male counterpart and usually paired with mermaid but he occasionally appears alone e.g. Anstey, Herts. (font); Chivelstone, Devon (screen); Queen Camel, Som. (boss). Both occur e.g. Beverley Minster, Yorks. (boss); Ripon, Yorks. (misericord); Stratford, Warks. (misericord); Sutcombe, Devon (bench-end).

MICHAEL, ST.   see also *Angels.*
Archangel (Rev. 12.7ff.) usually represented in armour with flaming sword, sometimes with motto (war-cry) inscribed: 'Quis ut Deus' – 'Who is like God?', a translation of the Hebrew Micha-el. He is supreme commander of the legions of angels who engage in unceasing warfare with the fallen angel Lucifer and his demon hosts ('the powers of the air'). Hence he is the patron of high places and many hill churches are dedicated to him such as Mount St. Michael, Roche, Cornw. e.g. Hoveringham, Notts. (tympanum); Martham, Norf. (glass); Moreton Valence, Glos. (tympanum); Sherborne, Dorset (boss); Tewkesbury, Glos. (boss); Wells cathedral (glass); Winterbourne Steepleton, Dorset (porch). He is also depicted weighing souls at the Last Day e.g. Catherington, Hants. (mural); Cliffe-at-Hoo, Kent (mural); East Wickham, Kent (mural); Eaton Bishop, Herefs. (glass); Martham, Norf. (glass); Ulcombe, Kent (mural).

St. Michael

MILL, MYSTIC   see also *Windmill.*
May symbolise the Mill of God which not only 'grinds exceeding small' but also represents the suffering involved in the transformation from earthly to heavenly state. Wheat is ground into flour which may become the body of Christ in the Eucharist. This sense goes back to C1 Ignatius of Antioch who desired to be ground into God's fine flour by the teeth of lions.

It also occurs as a complex symbol of the pure flour of the Gospel being separated from the obscuring husks of the Old Law by the stones of Christ's Incarnation and Passion. Christ's suffering has wrought the transformation which renders the bread of life available to the Gentiles.

MINISTRY OF CHRIST

Events in the earthly life of Christ (see also Infancy, Passion) include:

Good Samaritan: boss

Baptism: murals at Black Bourton, Oxon.; Brook, Kent; also on fonts.

Temptation: Brook, Kent (mural).

Marriage at Cana; East Harling, Norf. (glass).

Feet washed by Mary Magdalene, Mary sister of Martha, 'woman who was a sinner' (Lk. 7.37) who were all identified in Middle Ages: Leonard Stanley, Glos. (capital); West Horsley, Surrey (glass).

Raising Lazarus: Brook, Kent (mural); Lenton, Notts. (font).

Maundy (q.v.): Wiston, Suff. (carving);

Last Supper: Capel, Kent; Fairstead, Essex; Horsham, Sussex.

Parables are represented e.g. Dives and Lazarus (q.v.) Great Milton, Oxon. (glass); Good Samaritan, Ripon, Yorks. (boss); Findon, Sussex; Ulcombe, Kent (murals).

MIRACLES

Their possibility was part of mediaeval culture and faith. They loved and expected miracles as a sign that God had not abandoned the world to mere natural or mechanical order. They are attributed not only to God in Christ e.g. Chichester cathedral Sussex (relief) but to His saints e.g. Beverley minster, Yorks. (reredos); Brook, Kent (mural); Lincoln cathedral (boss and glass); Norwich cathedral (bosses); York, St. Denys Walmergate (glass).

MISERICORDS

Misericord

'Compassionate seats', so designed as to give some support to occupant when standing (especially during Night Offices). They provide a rich source of imagery: satirical, devotional, moral and decorative e.g. Croft, Hackness, Old Malton, Yorks. Subjects include:

Animal allegories: Beverley minster, Yorks.; Malvern, Worcs.; Manchester cathedral; Nantwich, Ches.

Biblical subjects: Ripon, Worcester cathedrals.

Domestic scenes: Beverley, Yorks.; Boston, Lincs.;
    Fairford, Glos.; Kings Lynn, Norf.; Minster,
    Kent; Windsor St. George, Berks.
Monsters: Wysall, Notts.
Moral exemplars: Edlesborough, Bucks.; Ludlow,
    Salop.; Stratford, Warks.
Natural life: Chester cathedral; Christchurch,
    Hants.; Winchester, Worcester cathedrals.
Religious topics: Ely cathedral; Gayton,
    Northants.; Lincoln cathedral.
Seasonal occupations: Screveton, Notts.
Saints: Sherborne, Dorset.
    There are also literary references (q.v.),
sports and pastimes (q.v.) conflicts (q.v.) foliate
heads (q.v.) and 'jeux d'esprit'.

MITRE   see *Vestments.*

MONOGRAMS
Occur on vestments and other embroidery,
carvings, painting e.g. East Harling, Norf. (screen);
glass (Thaxted, Essex). See *Initial Letters.*

MONSTERS   see also *Fabulous Beasts;*
Monster   *Giants; Grotesques.*
Monsters which devour people, other monsters,
and even the church fabric, are common and
symbolise the constant and insidious mordant
attacks of evil for which we must be alert.
Disorder is always tending to break in and destroy
the fragile order which has to be postively
maintained e.g. Upwell, Norf.

MONSTRANCE
Sacred vessel with a glass or crystal front for the
display of the Host in devotional services.

MONTHS   see also *Labours of . . ; Kalendar;*
Zodiac.
Months and seasons are common subjects for the
symbolic enrichment of doorways, fonts, glass,
misericords and tiles. The symbols relate to the
toil resulting from sin, earthly life, and the passing
of time. They may also indicate that Christ is the
Lord of Time.

MONUMENTS   see also *Brass; Burial;*
Hatchment; Memento Mori.
Monstrance   It has been observed that after the Reformation

Monument

inscriptions change from petition to God to praise of the departed, that imagery represents human pride rather than humility and that the effigies themselves tend to raise themselves from a recumbent to a standing position e.g. Bottesford, Leics.; Bramfield, Suff.; Eastrington, Yorks.; Fenny Bentley, Derbys.; Goldsborough, Ledsham, Skipton, Snaith, Yorks.; Strensham, Worcs.; Swine, tickhill, Yorks.; Wellington, Som.; Welwick, Yorks.; Yarnton, Oxon.

Rich imagery may be found on tomb-chests e.g. Harewood, Yorks.; Ross-on-Wye, Herefs.; Willoughby-on-Wolds, Notts.

MOSES
Law giver, moral authority, type of Christ. e.g. Evesham All Saints, Worcs. (carving); Twycross, Leics. (glass).

MOUTH OF HELL   see also *Harrowing of Hell.*
Hell was represented as entered through a monstrous mouth (whale ?). The image may be derived from the corrosive effect of sin (see Monsters) or from Jonah and the whale via the Mystery Plays e.g. Ashampstead, Berks. (mural); Barming, Kent (bench-end); Chaldon, Surrey; Cliffe-at-Hoo, Kent (murals); Horning, Norf. North Cray, Kent (bench-ends).

MURAL   see *Wall-painting.*

MUSIC
Central to popular mediaeval life and devotion: heaven was a place of music. Angels (q.v.) frequently bear musical instruments and there are plenty of human musicians in imagery e.g. bosses: Beverley St. Mary, Yorks.; Croscombe, Som.; Lincoln, Norwich, Wells, Winchester cathedrals; York All Saints (roof beams); as well as animal ones e.g. misericords at Boston, Lincs.; Ripon, Yorks.

Music

'In the Christian service, the actual sacrifice is no longer really performed, it is symbolised, transcendentalised, spiritualised. The service is a parable. So prayers and chants became the realities which had to be emphasised more and more; they too served the process of spiritualisation.'

Above all, music is a symbol of harmony and order as against dissonance and disorder. It has associations with Heaven, God's Kingdom, where the body and soul, mind and spirit of redeemed man are in Concert and attuned to the will of God. Wind music, especially when played by pigs, symbolised disordered passions and the ascendancy of animality over spirituality.

MYSTERY PLAYS   see also *Drama*.
Originated in the Easter Liturgy (see Easter Sepulchre) but soon developed and transferred from church to church yard and streets. Even country churches had their own play and some even had a natural amphitheatre for their performance e.g. St. Just, Cornwall. Mystery plays had a very powerful effect on both the matter and form of mediaeval church imagery.

Playing music

NATIVITY
The date of Christ's birth is unknown. From C4 it was celebrated on Dec. 25th in opposition to a sun festival, as the birth of the 'Sun of Righteousness' and this festival gradually replaced Old Christmas Day (Epiphany) in importance. Most of the traditional associations are mediaeval introductions: the wooden stable, the ox and ass e.g. Sandbach, Cheshire (Saxon crucifix). Representation was popularised by the devotion to the crib introduced by St. Francis in 1223 e.g. East Harling, Norf. (glass); Long Melford, Suff. (alabaster); Norwich St. Peter Mancroft (glass); Norwich St. Helen (boss); Worcester cathedral (carving). The Revelations of St. Bridget of Sweden (early C14) introduced the image of the Child lying on the stable floor emitting rays of glory (Malvern, Worcs – glass).

Nativity scene

NATURE
Love of and joy in nature is shown in the profusion of foliage carving, both conventional and naturalistic. The latter often shows the most accurate observation: oak with acorns and galls, maple with its winged seed, hawthorn and berries, vine and grapes, ranunculus, rue, wormwood and others, including the strangely popular water-lily. Some of these representations undoubtedly carry symbolic meaning but others have at least an element of direct response.

101

NEGRO

Occurs among Magi (q.v.) as representing one of the three races into which humankind was divided. But there seems to have been another inspiration which produced the tavern sign of 'The Negro's Head' and the boss in Exeter Lady Chapel.

NIMBUS   see *Halo*.

NOAH

Popular figure because his ark symbolised Church and baptism and because of his comic development in the mystery plays e.g. Malvern, Worcs. (glass); Norwich cathedral (boss); York St. Michael Spurriergate (glass).

Noah

NOBODIES

Common grotesque motif – heads with protruding limbs but no indication of a body. It may be derived from a Celtic head-cult but perhaps simply an expression of that deformity which is associated with evil and its effects e.g. Dorchester, Oxon.; Lowick, Northd. (capitals).

NOLI ME TANGERE   see also *Magdalene; Resurrection*.

'Touch me not' (John 20.11-18). Christ's appearance to Mary Magdalene in the garden (q.v.) was a popular subject (as was the Magdalen as an exemplar of God's complete forgiveness and the development of sexual attraction into love) e.g. bosses at Nantwich, Ches.; Norwich and Worcester cathedrals.

Trinity window

NUMBERS, SYMBOLIC

Believing that all things 'hung together' (idea of Great Chain of Being) and that therefore there was meaning in all things, the mediaevals found special significance in certain numbers and their associations:

1   Unity of God; integrity.
2   The two natures of Christ, human and divine; union; couple.
3   The Holy Trinity of Father, Son and Holy Spirit; the theological virtues of Faith, Hope and Charity (Love); three races of humankind.
4   The Gospels; cardinal virtues of Prudence,

Temperance, Fortitude, Justice; the Last Things – Death, Judgement, Heaven, Hell; Order; Completion; four orders of animal creation.

5 Wounds of Christ. Cinque-foil is a very common motif whose symbolism may be lost.

6 Attributes of the Godhead, eternity, impassibility, unchangeableness etc.

7 Includes: the days of creation; corporal works of mercy; deadly sins; sacraments; virtues; penitential psalms; joys, sorrows and glories of Mary; gifts of the Holy Spirit; Liberal Arts; the words from the Cross; the champions of Christendom: Saints George, Andrew, David, Patrick, Denis, James, Anthony; the outpourings of Christ's blood: circumcision, Gethsemane, scourging, crowning, hands, feet and side. Carries the general sense of completion, totality, perfection.

8 Re-creation; regeneration.

12 Apostles; Tribes of Israel.

40 Days of the flood; years in the wilderness and of bondage to the Philistines; days of Moses' sojourn on the mount and Elijah's concealment; of Jonah's preaching and Christ's fasting. Sanctuary lasted for forty days and there could be forty days of rain after St. Swithun's day. There were devotions of forty hours and forty days.

Complexity could be increased by combination or factorisation. Thus twelve is three times four, fourteen is twice seven (see Fourteen Holy Helpers) and one hundred and forty-four is the square of twelve (Rev. 21.17 etc.). Such processes combined or increased the symbolisation.

OFFERTORY BOXES   see also *Alms; Peter's Pence.*
In the Middle Ages these were normally connected with a particular devotion, shrine etc. Some stone ones survive e.g. Bridlington, Speeton, Wensley, Yorks. Portable boxes used during services are a post-Reformation introduction; early examples survive e.g. Blickling, Norf.; Blythburgh, Suff.; Chelmorton, Derbys.; Coneysthorpe, Yorks.; Guildford Holy Trinity; Kirkby Stephen, Westm.; Kirkoswald, Cumb.

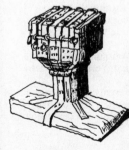

Offertory box

The offering of money is a symbol, and usually a commutation, of sacrifice (Mark 12.42).

OFFICE   see *Divine Office; Hours.*

OIL, HOLY
In the Old Testament prophets, priests, kings and sacred objects were anointed to symbolise their consecration to the Divine service. 'Christ' means 'The Anointed One'. Chrism is a mixture of olive oil and balsam used in the sacraments (q.v.) of Baptism, Confirmation and Holy Orders symbolising the fulness of sacramental grace, the gifts of the Spirit and the fragrance of virtue. Other oils are used for the anointing of the sick and at the blessing of the font. A chrismatory is a vessel to hold the three types of holy oil. Oil in general is a symbol of strength, joy and dedication.

Container for
Holy Oils

OLD TESTAMENT   see also *Types.*
Representations of Old Testament events as prefiguring those of the New are frequent in carving, glass and paint. Subjects include:
Moses, often depicted with horns due to a
    mistranslation: Holcombe Rogus, Devon;
    North Tuddenham, Suff.; Southrop, Glos.;
    Stamford St. Martin, Lincs.; Worcester
    cathedral.
Spies returning from Canaan (Numbers 13):
    Beverley minster, Yorks.; Milverton, Som.;
    Twycross, Leics.
Balaam's ass (Numbers 22): Holcombe Rogus,
    Devon.
Gideon's fleece (Judges 6.36-40): Fairford, Glos.
David: Bradninch, Devon.; Highworth, Wilts.;
    Norwich cathedral; Sherborne, Dorset.;
    Stamford St. Martin, Lincs.; York St. Martin-
    cum-Gregory.
Solomon: Fairford, Glos.; Westminster Henry VII
    chapel; Worcester cathedral; York St. Michael
    Spurriergate.
    The symbolism of these events can be obscure
e.g. Gideon's fleece refers to the Virgin Birth and the Visit of the Queen of Sheba to the conversion of heathen.

Spies

OPUS DEI   see also *Hours.*
'Work for God' i.e. the recitation of the canonical

hours, prime duty of monks. St. Benedict's motto was 'Work is prayer and prayer work'.

ORGAN

Introduced to England by C8. Oldest surviving case is at Old Radnor, Flints. Symbol of praise that Church continually offers to God. Attribute of St. Cecilia, patron of musicians, who is the legendary inventor of the organ to express the flood of harmony which filled her soul.

Organ

ORIENTATION

'The foundation must be so contrived that the Head of the church may point due East, i.e. to that point of the heavens wherein the sun arises at the equinoxes – to signify that the Church Militant must behave herself with moderation both in prosperity and adversity – and not towards that point where the sun arises at the solstices.' (Durandus).

The sun is a common symbol of Christ and the Church, both physical and spiritual, must be directed towards Him.

The orientation of some English churches seems to be directed to the point of sunrise on the patronal festival.

The South is the area of the sun, the realm of Christ, and therefore churchyards lie towards the South side of the church and are often on the South side of the original village they served. The North side of the churchyard was of ill-repute and often served for the burial of criminals, suicides and the unbaptised.

ORNAMENTS, ECCLESIASTICAL   see also *Liturgical Colours.*

Include vestments, furniture and fittings as well as purely decorative items. Their traditional purpose was that 'through visible, we might be led to invisible beauty' (Durandus). Mediaeval colours had symbolic significance: white – purity, single-mindedness; red – charity, divine love; green - contemplation, growth (spiritual); black – mortification of the flesh, self-discipline; livid colours – tribulation.

OUR LADY, LIFE OF   see also *Virgin Mary.*

Devotion to Our Lady was characteristic of

mediaeval life and culture and she represented
the human and feminine element in spiritual
life. Her legendary parents were Joachim and
Anne and there are many representations of Our
Lady and St. Anne in a 'spiritual education'
context e.g. York All Saints (glass). The main
subjects of contemplative devotion were
enshrined in her 'mysteries' (see Rosary) and
those most frequently represented (with the
exception of Madonna, q.v.) are her Coronation
(the triumph of a totally human personality)
and her Assumption (the resurrection of a
totally human being). The form of much
Marian, as other, iconography was greatly
influenced by the Mystery Plays.

PAINTING   see also *Wall Painting*.

Painting, symbolic, naturalistic or decorative
occurred on ceilings, vaults, walls and window
splays, on the panels of screens, pulpits, tombs;
in short, on every surface. Not only was sculpture
painted but even the entire exterior of buldings.
The coloured edifice, so frequently seen in
miniatures (which use the same forms as the
architecture), was not a creation of the artist's
fancy but a representation of the familiar aspect
of buildings.

PALL

1. Stiffened linen cloth with which chalice is
covered at Eucharist, symbolising (together with
corporal), the grave clothes of Christ.
2. Coffin or hearse (q.v.) covering usually of
white, black or purple velvet or other rich stuff.
Each church had a parochial one but religious
fraternities and noble families had their own
e.g. Dunstable, Beds.; Sudbury St Peter, Suff.

PALM SUNDAY

Sunday before Easter, introduction of Holy
Week. Its distinctive features are the blessing of
palms and the procession which represents
Christ's triumphal entry into Jerusalem
(Matthew 21.1-11). Often a special gallery was
built at the main entrance of the church to
accommodate the choir for the anthem: 'Gloria,
laus et honor'. Traces of this gallery at Aylsham,
Cawston, Norf.; Kingston Seymour, Som.;
Westbury-on-Trym, Glos.; Weston-in-Gordano,

Palm Sunday

Som.; Worstead, Norf. Representations of entry into Jerusalem and/or Palm Sunday e.g. Aston Eyre, Salop. (tympanum); Malvern, Worcs. (glass); West Haddon, Northants. (font).

PASCHAL CANDLE

Easter candle (Pasch=Passover=Easter). A large candle on a special stand (often richly wrought and decorated) at the north side of the sanctuary. It is blessed and lit on Easter Eve and extinguished on Ascension Day after the Gospel. It symbolises Christ's bodily presence on earth after the Resurrection and the five grains of incense fixed in it represent the Five Wounds (q.v.). It is an ancient Christian belief that earthly wounds received for righteousness' sake become emblems of glory.

PASSION (SUFFERING) OF CHRIST

The central object of personal and communal devotion during the later Middle Ages, symbolised in the great rood, the Good Friday Liturgy, emblems of the Instruments of the Passion, the Five Wounds etc.

'In their detailed descriptions of the agony on the Cross or the earlier Passion scenes, in which the suffering Redeemer is made to appeal directly to the audience, our English preachers of C14-15 approach nearest to the tender sweetness of the love-lyric' (Owst) e.g. Almondbury, Yorks. (screen inscription); Brook, Kent.; Easby, Yorks.; Fairstead, Essex; Little Missenden, Bucks.; West Chiltington, Sussex. For specific episodes, e.g. Agony in garden: Bosbury, Herefs.; Ford, Sussex; Shorthampton, Oxon. Crowning with thorns: Norwich St Peter Mancroft; Tiverton, Devon. Carrying Cross: Blunham, Beds.; Leek, Staffs.; Yarnton, Oxon. Nailing: Auckland, Durham; Norwich cathedral transept; Stockerston, Leics.

Crucifixion: Coleshill, Warks.; Drayton Parsloe, Bucks.; East Harling, Norf.; Hingham, Norf.; Honington, Suff.; Langford, Oxon.; Lenton, Notts.; Sall, Norf.; Stoke D'Abernon, Surrey.

Legend of the Cross: Ashton-under-Lyne, Lancs.; East Harling, Norf.; Morley, Derbys.; St Neot, Cornw.

Paschal candle

Passion of Christ

Passion emblems

Patron Saint

PASSIONTIDE
Liturgical season from fifth Sunday in Lent to
Good Friday.

PASSION EMBLEMS
Include Heart with crown of thorns e.g. Fowey,
Cornw. (boss); Five Wounds (q.v.) e.g. North
Cadbury, Som. (bench-end) but particularly
Instruments of the Passion (q.v.).

PATEN   see *Vessels, sacred.*

PATRON SAINTS   see also *Saints, Fourteen Holy Helpers.*
The mediaeval belief in the credal article 'the
Communion of Saints' was practical and realistic.
They found holy supporters and intercessors for
every need and purpose, not only of individuals
but of churches, cities, countries, corporations
and guilds. Whether as an individual or as a
member of a group, Everyman was assured of the
support of heavenly advocates. The assumption
of a Christian name automatically placed him
under the protection of his name-saint and he
could gain support by adopting others. The
patron saint of a church was usually elevated on
a bracket or a niche on the south side of the
high altar and other representations occurred in
chapels, over porches or on towers. Guilds and
other corporations often found their patron
through associations which to a modern mind
might seem remote or irrelevant. To take the
single case of St. John the Baptist; he was
patron of the wool-trade, domestic animals and
their keepers because of his attribute of the
Agnus Dei; of those working with cloth,
leather or pelts because of his clothing; of those
who worked with sharp-edged tools (including
cutlers and carpenters) because of his beheading;
of awl- and needle-workers because of the legend
that Herodias pierced his head with a pin; of
chandlers because he was called 'a light'(Lk. 1.79);
of solitaries and bird-catchers because of his long
imprisonment. Other craft patrons included:
Barbara for gunners, Bartholomew for surgeons,
Cecilia for musicians, Catherine for schools,
Cosmas and Damien (and Luke) for physicians,
Crispin and Crispinian for shoemakers, Eloi for
farriers, Eustace and Hubert for huntsmen, John

Arms of St. Edward

the Evangelist for paper-makers and book-binders, Luke for painters, Nicholas for bankers, pawnbrokers and sailors, Neot for scarecrows and Thomas for masons.

There were 'therapeutic' saints: Apollonia for toothache, Blaise for throat ailments, Erasmus for bowel complaints, Hubert for rabies, Giles for cripples, Lazarus for lepers and Roche for plague and there were what we might call 'state of life' patrons: Christopher for the common man, George for knights, Giles for beggars, Leonard for prisoners, Lucy for peasants, Petronilla for servants and Nicholas for children.

PATRONAL FESTIVAL   see *Dedication*.

PAX

The 'kiss of peace' was an important part of Mass ceremony, signifying the unity and love of the brethren. In C13 the direct kiss was replaced by the 'pax' or 'osculatorium', a tablet (usually of precious metal) bearing a crucifix which was kissed first by the senior cleric then, in order, it was kissed by all the ministers and passed from the sanctuary to the congregation whence it returned to the altar, symbolising Christ the source and model of Christian charity. A very rare survival e.g. Oxford All Souls, Oxford New College.

PETER'S PENCE   see also *Alms*.

From C8 English Catholics made a special contribution to central Church funds called St. Peter's Pence since Rome was held to be the See of Peter. In C12 Henry II promised 'an English penny every year to Rome for every chimney that gave forth smoke in England'. Special collecting boxes seem to have been provided for this purpose e.g. Nettleton, Wilts,; Sandwich St. Mary, Kent.

Pew end

PEWS   see also *Seats*.

General congregational seating developed from C15 and the wooden benches were elaborated with carved bench-ends (q.v.) sometimes possessing finial (see Poppy Head). The carving is often didactic e.g. seven deadly sins (Wiggenhall St. Mary, Norf.): seven sacraments (Wiggenhall St. German, Norf.); or represents local trade by

Pew carving

windmills, ships or tools e.g. Altarnum, Cornw.;
Broomfield, Som.; Fressingfield, Suff.; Harpley,
Norf.; High Bickington, Devon.; Woolpit, Norf. All
aspects of life, faith, morals, work, are bonded
together in the Church. The triumph of the
Protestant ethic at the Reformation led to the
rapid growth of private and lockable pews. The
squire's pew often had the size (and sometimes
the location) of the old chantry chapel e.g.
Wensley, Yorks.; Whalley, Lancs. The apogee
was reached when such pews became roofed with
canopies and testers, fitted with fireplaces and
cupboards and supplied with food and drink.

'A bedstead of the antique mode,
Compact of timber many a load,
Such as our ancestors did use
Was metamorphosed into pews;
Which still their ancient nature keep
By lodging folks disposed to sleep.' (Swift)

e.g. Baswich, Staffs.; Ellingham, Hants.; Madley,
Herefs.; Stokesay, Salop.; Tevershall, Notts.

PHALLIC SYMBOLS   see also *Horn; Sheila-na-gig.*

Probably occurred with some frequency in the
Middle Ages, rare survivals due to inaccessibility
e.g. bosses at Beverley St. Mary, Yorks.;
Worcester cathedral nave.

PIETA

Dead Christ in the arms of His mother e.g. Bag
Enderby, Lincs. (font); Battlefield, Salop.
(statue); Breadsall, Derbys. (alabaster);
Broughton, Bucks.; Corby, Lincs. (murals).
Long Melford, Suff. (glass); Orford, Suff. (font).

PILGRIMS   see also *Cross (Tau).*

Characteristic of Middle Ages expressing belief
in sacred time and place and also emphasising
that entire life is a pilgrimage. Christ is the
exemplary Pilgrim ascending from earth to
heaven via the demanding Way of the Cross
and He is sometimes depicted as a pilgrim in
the episode on the road to Emmaus (Luke
24.13ff.) e.g. Fairford, Glos. (glass). St. James,
their patron, is usually depicted in pilgrim dress:
broad-brimmed hat, the emblem of his shrine at
Compostella (scallop-shell), and a staff with a

Pilgrim

hook for the scrip (water-bottle) e.g. Bere Regis, Dorset.; Edlesborough, Bucks.; Normanton, Yorks. There is a possible die for the manufacture of pilgrims' badges at Pirton, Worcs.

PISCINA

Drain, with direct access into consecrated ground, for the disposal of water used for washing hands before Consecration and rinsing vessels after Communion in ceremonies of Mass. It may double as credence (q.v.) and is often associated with sedilia (q.v.). It provides useful evidence of a vanished altar.

Piscinas are very common, if not universal e.g. Aconbury, Hunts.; Barton-le-Street, Yorks.; Bunney, Notts.; Compton Beauchamp, Berks.; Grantham, Lincs.; Horwood, Devon; Long Wittenham, Berks.; Rothwell, Northants.; Stratford Toney, Wilts.; York Holy Trinity Goodramgate.

The changes in form from single to double, back to single and their final disappearance in modern Catholic churches is due to changes in the ceremonial of Mass reflecting doctrinal development. '

Piscina

PITY, CHRIST OF

Image of resurrected Christ bearing crown of thorns and prominent wounds. It was an extremely popular and heavily indulged object of late mediaeval devotion, associated with the Mass of St. Gregory (q.v.), e.g. Banwell, Som. (boss); Diddington, Hunts. (glass); Fairford, Glos. (exterior carving); Fingrinhoe, Essex (mural); Herstmonceux, Sussex (brass); Macclesfield, Chesh. (brass); Peterborough cathedral porch, (boss); Roxton, Beds. (screen).

POOR BOX   see *Alms*.

POPPY HEAD

Carved termination of benches which generally takes the form of a trefoil of close-knit foliage (symbolising Trinity?) but it may be developed into animal or human figures, often with symbolic significance e.g. Balderton, Notts.; South Burlingham, Norf.; Stanton St. John, Oxon.

Poppy head

111

Porch

Hands in prayer
position

PORCH

Important part of church and the location of ecclesiastical functions (churching, marriage, penance) as well as secular (signing of contracts, schooling). It may contain an altar (or its remains), a 'witnessing' statue (or its empty plinth or niche) e.g. Bampton, Oxon.; Buckland, Berks.; Eye, Suff.; Yateley, Hants. A chamber over could accommodate a priest, relics or parish treasure, a school or even the town council (Cirencester, Glos.). The mediaeval secular use explains the contemporary display of local government notices etc.

Porch decoration was often related to the notion of Christ as Door e.g. Majestas: Elkstone, Glos.; Pedmore, Worcs.; Rowlstone, Herefs.; Water Stratford, Bucks.
Madonna: Fownhope, Herefs.; Inglesham, Wilts.; Northleach, Glos.
The Agnus Dei, Tree of Life and Cross are extremely frequent e.g. Bradford-on-Avon, Wilts.; Headbourne Worthy, Hants.; Langford, Oxon.

Other porch decorations included apostles, patron saint, St. Michael or St. George e.g. Thorverton, Devon (boss).

PRAYERS

Mediaeval prayers survive on windows, memorials and sometimes other furniture such as bell, font, pulpit. They usually ask for, or express, prayers for the repose of the donor. There are suffrages to the Trinity, to individual Persons of the Godhead, and invocations of saints (especially Virgin Mary). Most are in Latin, some in English, all tend to be short e.g. 'Jesus mercy', 'Mary help', 'Jesus be a Saviour to me!' Later inscribed prayers tend to be prolix, literary and self-conscious with strong Biblical references. They do not ask for other's prayers.

PRAYERS FOR THE DEAD   see also
Chantry.
An ancient Christian practice that grew considerably as a result of the developed doctrine of Purgatory as an intermediate state between death and Heaven. Masses and other prayers for the dead were considered as alms deeds for which many instiutions were

founded e.g. Beauchamp chapel, Warwick;
Henry VII chapel, Westminster; All Souls
College, Oxford. The Reformers regarded prayers
for the dead superstitious and the doctrine of
Purgatory vain and therefore abolished some
three thousand institutions with the responsibility
of praying for their founders, including schools,
hospitals, hospices and almshouses. There is a
unique 'Poor Souls' Light' in church yard at
Bisley, Glos. and a possible variant form in porch
at Aldsworth, Glos.

PREACHING   see also *Sermon; Pulpit*.
Mediaeval homiletics were structured round the
Apostles' Creed (Faith), the Commandments,
virtues and vices (Behaviour), and the Lord's
Prayer and Ave Maria (Spirituality). Their verbal
exposition was supported and echoed by graphic
images in painting, sculpture and glass. 'Images
are poor men's books' and there is evidence
that the preacher appealed directly to the
examples and illustrations depicted all round
his audience. The central subject of preaching
was Christ crucified: the dominant Great Rood,
the crucifix over the pulpit and often a crucifix
in the hands of the preacher e.g. Winchester
cathedral Lady-chapel (bench-end).

PRIDE
The chiefest and most deadly of the deadly sins
according to mediaeval moral teaching. Its
essence is self-reference rather than God-reference.
Like all the deadly sins, it is seminal and the
source of other sins; for instance misdirected
curiosity was seen as a species of pride. It is a
frequent subject for imagery and its symbols
include tiger, mermaid, trumpet, bagpipes,
Death and the Maiden, a knight fallen from his
horse. Lucifer fell through pride and moralists
call Pride his eldest daughter (see Daughters of
God). e.g. Hoxne, Suffolk; Ruislip, Middlesex
(paintings).

Pride

PROFANE LOVE
Part of life and therefore part of church imagery
e.g. Kilpeck, Herefs. (corbel); Exeter, Lincoln,
Norwich cathedrals (bosses); Raunds, Northants.
(mural); Wiggenhall St. German, Norf. (benches).
Most representations seem to be warnings

against lechery. None of the erotic sculpture which survives in some French churches seems to have done so in England (if it existed).

PROPHETS   see also *Apostles; Jesse.*
Prophets are seen as foretelling the mysteries of Christ and the articles of the Christian faith and are therefore usually associated with the Creed e.g. Arundel, Sussex (boss); Ashton, Devon (screen); Bridford, Devon (screen); Capel, Kent (mural); Fairford, Glos. (glass); Lincoln cathedral choir (boss); Madley, Herefs. (glass); Southwold, Suff. (screen); Tewkesbury, Glos. (glass).

PULPIT
Originally a raised platform from which to declaim, hence 'pulpitum' means the cathedral rood-screen from which the Gospel was sung. Now the word is applied to the raised enclosure, occupied by a preacher, often with a sounding board and sometimes an hour-glass. The 'three-decker' pulpit was a post-Reformation development, combining stalls for minister and clerk with a pulpit e.g. Minstead, Hants.; Sall, Norf.; Whitby, Yorks.; York, Holy Trinity.

Pulpit

The mediaevals expected learning and the transmission of traditional doctrine from the preacher since he was the intermediary between the theologians and the laity. Hence pulpits are decorated with figures of doctors (q.v.) e.g. Burnham Norton, Norf.; Trull, Som. or of saints e.g. Kenton, Halberton, Tor Bryan, Devon, or of evangelists e.g. Affpuddle, Dorset, or apostles e.g. Long Sutton, Som., or of canonised preachers e.g. Frampton-on-Frome, Dorset.

The Reformation continued the emphasis on preaching and so the iconography continued too e.g. Stoke St. Gregory, Som.; Giggleswick, Yorks.

Some mediaeval pulpits were moveable and served for occasional sermons in chapels or before 'preaching cross' of the kind that still exist e.g. Blackfriars Cross, Hereford; Iron Acton, Glos. Fixed mediaeval pulpits survive e.g. in wood at Castle Acre, Norf.; Rossington, Yorks. and in stone e.g. Witheridge, Devon (with carved rood).

The post-Reformation moveable pulpit at Kirkington, Notts. had occasional extra-mural use as a 'hide' for a C19 duck-shooting rector.

PYX

Receptacle of wood, precious metal or ivory for the reservation of the Blessed Sacrament, suspended over the High Altar from a pulley and raised or lowered from a locked aumbry in the chancel. The pyx was usually in the form of a dove which was veiled out of reverence. A mediaeval veil survives at Hessett, Suff.; the pulley-socket at West Grinstead, Sussex; a pyx at Warkleigh, Devon and a pyx-cover at Dennington, Suff. Sometimes the sacrament was reserved in an aumbry or in a small locker or tabernacle on the altar (as in contemporary Catholic practice).

Pyx canopy

QUIRE   see *Church Symbolism.*

Alternative spelling of 'choir' but useful to distinguish that part of the church beyond the nave in contradistinction to the body of singers who often occupy part of this area.

RABBIT, HARE, CONEY   see also *Animals.*

Three rabbits sharing three ears seems a common device in Dartmoor area e.g. Broadclyst, Chagford, North Bovey, Sampford Courtney, South Tawton, Spreyton, Tavistock, Widecombe-in-the-Moor, Devon (bosses). There is a similar arrangement on a boss at Selby, Yorks. with a disconnected fourth rabbit. The same device occurs in glass e.g. Long Melford, Suff. and at Paderborn, Germany and therefore it appears to have symbolic significance and probably refers to the Trinity.

REALISM

Realism: playing a ball game

Perhaps more of a mediaeval characteristic than the mysticism romantically attributed to the period. Sermons are full of the raw and simple facts of everyday life, direct, candid, forceful. Imagery gives the same impression with its representations of seed-time and harvest, summer and winter, the stars in their course, familiar social types, flora and fauna, peddlers and fradulent inn-keepers, the pot boiling over the fire, the ubiquitous house-dog, knights and monks, bear-baiting and hunting, towns and buildings, builder's square and scholar's book.

Rebus

Rebus

REBUS

A heraldic device making a kind of visual pun e.g. doe on a tun for 'Donnington' (Beverley minster, Yorks.), three gilded stones under a mitre for Abbot Goldstone (Canterbury cathedral, boss); others: John Ashburton at Baunton, Glos. (altar-frontal); James Cockerell at Guisborough, Yorks. (tomb); Henry Thistleton at Ketteringham, Norf. (glass).

RECUMBENT EFFIGIES   see *Knights and Ladies.*

RELICS   see also *Reliquary.*

From its earliest days, the church venerated the corpses of its martyrs (Rev. 1.6), erecting memorials over their tombs, using the tomb as an altar or orientating a memorial church so that its high altar was over the saint's grave. This attitude sprang from a very realistic concept of the psychosomatic nature of man and an almost physical notion of the nature of goodness and its transmission.

Relics became a source of profit and sometimes both the object acquired and the means of its acquisition were alike dubious. The bodies or fragments of bodies attributed to saints were enclosed in costly reliquaries (q.v.) which rested in aumbries, crypts and shrines and attracted countless pilgrims. Both the superstitions attached to them and the wealth associated with them made shrines a target for reforming zeal and few relics remain. However, St. Edward remains at Westminster, Cuthbert and Bede at Durham and St. Candida at Whitchurch Canonicorum, Dorset. The tympanum of Little Bytham, Lincs. is said to have enclosed a relic of St. Medard, patron of the church.

One of the pillars at Pewsey, Wilts. seems to contain a relic of 'angels' feathers'.

RELIGIOUS ORDERS   see also *Hermits.*

Groups living under rule ('regulars' from Latin for 'rule'), having taken life-long vows of poverty, chastity and obedience. The chief orders affecting the architecture and iconography of the Church are:

monks:

Benedictines, (f.525 A.D.), the 'Black Monks'

Religious orders

e.g. brasses at Cowfold, Sussex; Norwich St. Lawrence; effigy at Bodmin, Cornw.; Peterborough cathedral; Ramsey Abbey gatehouse, Hunts. Cistercians, (f. 1098), the 'White Monks' e.g. mural at Hayles, Glos.

Monks and nuns were, ideally, enclosed and remained in their convents. (effigy of abbess at Polesworth, Warks.)

friars:

Franciscans (f.1210), the 'Grey Friars' or 'Friars Minor'. Dominicans (f.1221), the 'Black Friars' or 'Friars Preacher'. Friars exercised their ministry outside their convents and were particularly active in preaching.

Besides monks and friars (who included lay brothers) there were communities of priests who exercised a sort of group ministry e.g.

Augustinian Canons (f.C12), 'the Black Canons' or 'Austin Canons' who were also involved in hospital service e.g. St. Bartholomew's, St. Thomas', London.

Besides the stricter 'regulars', other groups of parish clergy often lived a common or collegiate life as well as non-parochial clergy engaged in social and education work. Tertiaries were lay-folk formally attached to a mendicant order who kept its spirit and a modified form of its rule e.g. Conington, Hunts. (effigy).

Vowesses were widows who kept faith with their husbands by retiring to a convent e.g. brasses: Frenze, Norf.; Lower Quinton, Glos.; Shalston, Bucks.; Witton, Norf.

Reliquary

RELIQUARY   see also *Altar/Sepulchre*. Container for relics (q.v.) e.g. Shipley, Sussex; Wensley, Yorks., sometimes in the shape of that part of the body whose fragments they contained. As early as C4 Christians were contemptuously called 'Cinericii' ('remains men') but the practice of veneration of relics was defended as natural and analogous to preserving and respecting other remains belonging to the loved dead such as pictures and personal possessions. The practice also testified to the sanctity and importance of the body in opposition to the 'spiritualist' tradition which regarded it as a transitory encumbrance to the soul.

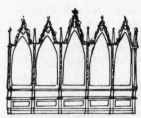

Reredos

REREDOS

Ornament behind altar to emphasise its importance. It may be painted directly on to the wall or take the form of a window or a hanging, but commonly it was painted on carved wooden or stone panels (see Alabaster). The central subject is almost invariably the Crucifixion. e.g. Bampton, Oxon.; Bunbury, Ches.; Drayton, Berks.; Great Canfield, Essex; Long Melford, Suff.; Norwich cathedral; Norwich St. George Tombland; Patrington, Yorks.; Ranworth, Norf.; Somerton, Oxon.; Stow, Lincs.; Thornham Parva, Suff.; Wells St. Cuthbert; Youlgreave, Derbys. Modern examples at: Burghwallis, Cantley, Harrogate St. Wilfrid, High Melton, Yorks.; Wymondham, Norf.

REQUIEM

Mass for dead (from opening words 'Requiem aeternam'–'Eternal rest'), characterised by black vestments, unbleached candles, omission of Gloria, blessing etc. as sign of mourning. The traditional month for remembering the dead is November which opens with the feast of All Saints, followed by the commemoration of All Souls.

RESURRECTION see also *Easter Sepulchre; Noli mi Tangere.*

The Resurrection of Christ is the source of Christian faith (I Cor. 15.4) and the pledge that man can be totally restored. The general resurrection is portrayed on Dooms (q.v.). The iconography of Christ's Resurrection shows Him naked, with manifest wound-scars and carrying triumphal banner (Vexillum q.v.). Subject occurs on Easter sepulchres and elsewhere e.g. Bishops Hull, Som. (bench-end); Fairford, Glos. (glass); Lenton, Notts. (font); Norwich cathedral cloisters (boss); West Chiltington, Sussex (mural); Wiston, Suff. (mural); Wrangle, Lincs. (glass); Wroxeter, Salop. (mural).

Other post-Resurrection appearances at Brook, Capel, Kent (murals); Easby, Yorks. (mural); Hawton, Notts. (sepulchre); Launcells, Cornw. (bench-end); Lincoln cathedral (misericord); Slimfold, Sussex (mural); West Harnham, Wilts. (mural); York All Saints (glass).

Jonah: resurrection

REVERENCE
In accordance with Christian concept of man inward reverence is symbolised by a variety of external acts: bowing, covering and uncovering head, genuflection, kneeling, prostration, standing, turning Eastwards, silence, making the sign of the cross etc.

RIDDEL   see *Altar Furniture*.

R.I.P.
'Requiescat in pace' – 'May he/she rest in peace'. The commonest prayer for the dead. Paradise is seen as a place of refreshment and rest, an endless Sabbath, after the toils and spiritual struggles of the working week which was life on earth.

Rogation

ROGATION TIDE
From the Latin for 'to ask'. Days of prayer and fasting in early summer with the special intention for a good harvest which included procession through the fields of the parish. It probably originated as a Christian version of the Roman 'Robiglia' on March 25th. e.g. Blythburgh, Suff. (bench-end); Ripple, Worcs.; Worcester cathedral (misericords).

ROOD

The cross of Christ, crucifix (from Old English for 'wood'). Dominant symbol of atonement, reunion of God and man embracing all creation. It was often flanked by the figures of Virgin Mary and St. John (John 19.26) representing the attendant Church. It was of universal occurrence, appearing on bench-ends, fonts, frontals, altar and processional crosses, paintings and carvings, preaching and church yard crosses – on almost any appropriate surface or object e.g. Barton-on-Humber, Lincs. (window mullions); Weston, Yorks. (back of cresset); Witheridge, Devon (pulpit panel).

Every mediaeval church was dominated by the Great Rood on its beam above the chancel arch or mounted on the chancel screen, hence called the Rood screen (q.v.). This Rood was honoured with candles and lights and when it had a loft this was used as an appropriate pulpit from which to read the Gospel (Good News). Some of these Roods have been restored in the last

119

Rood beam

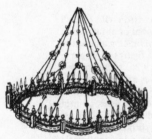

Corona lucis

century e.g. Campsall, Yorks.; Morley, Derbys.
This dominating image was intended 'to teach
us that we must love the Redeemer from the
midst of our hearts. . .and that all, seeing the
sign of victory, might exclaim "Hail, Thou
salvation of the whole world, Tree of our
Redemption" and that we should never forget
the love of God who, to redeem His servants,
gave His only Son, that we might imitate Him
crucified. The Cross is exalted on high to
signify the victory of Christ'. (Durandus).
Fragments of Christus from Great Rood at
South Cerney, Glos.; Cartmel, Lancs.

ROOD BEAM
Beam across front of chancel arch to support
great Rood (q.v.). Often destroyed with Rood at
Reformation but supporting corbels may
survive e.g. High Ham, Som.; Potter Heigham,
Norf.

ROOD LOFT
Platform above rood screen (q.v.) usually
reached by spiral stairs which may survive when
loft has been destroyed. It provided a place for
reading the Gospel at Mass and sometimes for
the altar of the Holy Rood and even for a choir
organ and some choristers. It always provided
for candles and lights and access for fitting
Lenten veil etc. After the Sacrament Light, the
Rood-light was the most important in the
mediaeval church. The front of the loft or the
upper surface of the Rood-beam (sometimes
called the 'candle-beam') always supported a
special lamp or 'great taper' immediately in
front of the Rood which was supplemented by
individual bequests and augmented at great
festivals. The Rood-light sometimes took the
form of a circular chandelier ('wheel' or 'crown')
holding between a dozen and a score lamps or
tapers. Pulley fittings for raising and lowering
this light survive e.g. Ubbeston, Wisset, Suff.
Examples of wooden lofts at Attleborough,
Norf.; Flamborough, Yorks.; of stone at
Christchurch, Hants.; Dunstable, Beds.; Howden,
Yorks.; of stairs at Hartland, Devon; Little
Rissington, Glos.; Sleaford, Lincs. and of stair-
turrets at Long Melford, Suff. The Rood loft at
Wouldham, Kent has a unique indirect approach.

Rood screen

Rood stone

ROOD SCREEN

In Western Europe, England was pre-eminent in the dominance of the rood screen as a liturgical feature and its surviving examples are the most numerous and beautiful, whether executed in wood or in stone, e.g. Aysgarth, Burghwallis, Yorks.; Compton, Surrey; Compton Bassett, Wilts.; Eye, Suff.; Hexham, Northd.; Kirkstead, Lincs.; Methley, Yorks.; Northfleet, Kent; Silkstone, Yorks.; Stanton Harcourt, Oxon.; Thurcaston, Leics.; Westhall, Suff.

The screen's horizontal top was usually dominated by foliage-carving of vine, wheat or oak which was often interspersed with birds or animals. The panels in the lower section were painted and pictures survive e.g. Ashton, Bradninch, Devon; Cawston, Norf.; South Pool, Devon. Small pierced openings appear in the lower section e.g. Bradwell, Essex; Hessett, Suff.; Mautby, Norf.; Rye, Sussex; South Leigh, Oxon.; Wintringham, Yorks. These have been explained as either grilles for confession or (more likely) apertures to facilitate sight of the Elevation of the Host during Mass.

Sometimes a canopy was built over the Rood to give it extra dignity and honour (see *Celure*) or the roof above was specially painted and gilded e.g. Sall, Norf.; Woolpit, Suff.

ROOD STONE

Monolith with carved or incised crucifix. Probably originated as a pagan cult-object which was converted by marking it with the Christian sign e.g. Lanherne (Mawgan), Cornw.; Rudston ('Rood-stone'), Yorks. Such stones should be related to Anglo-Saxon, butter and church yard crosses which together symbolise the consecration of all places and activities. Crosses survive on remote upland paths acting as a double sign-post (physical and spiritual) and perhaps also intended to give supernatural protection in high and lonely places.

ROOF

The church roof, especially that of the chancel, symbolised the sky and the glories of heaven. It was often coloured blue with gold stars and, when vaulted, its bosses were enriched with symbolic carvings e.g. Muchelney, Som. Hammer and tie beams were frequently adorned with carved angels playing music or bearing symbolic objects e.g. Addlethorpe, Lince.; Astbury, Ches.; Badingham, Suff.; Bere Regis, Dorset; Blakeney, Norf.; Blythburgh, Suff.; Bruton, Som.; Cullompton, Devon; Earl Stonham, Suff.; Evercreech, Som.; Grundisburgh, Hemingham, Suff.; Mark, Som.; Mildenhall, Suff.; Norwich St. Peter Hungate; Shepton Mallet, Som.; Thirsk, Yorks.; Ufford, Suff.; Upwell, Norf.; Watchet, Wellow, Wells St. Cuthbert, Som.; Whissendine, Rutl.; Woolpit, Suff.; Worlingworth.; York All Saints.

ROOF BOSS

Roof boss

Keystone at the intersection of vaulting. Most are carved with great care and detail even when distance makes them virtually invisible. The decoration became so important that bosses were retained in wooden roofs when there was no structural necessity e.g. Beverley St. Mary, Yorks.; Bruton, Som.; Lutterworth, Leics.; North Cadbury, Som. Because of their obscurity and inaccessibility bosses have usually escaped both the fury of iconoclasts and the ignorance of restorers and provide a rich repository of mediaeval art and symbolism e.g. Cricklade St. Sampson, Wilts.; Northwich, Ches.; Steeple Ashton, Tisbury, Wilts.; Wixford, Warks.

ROSARY

Rosary

Combines rose-symbolism with a method of meditative prayer in which fifteen decades of 'Aves', each decade preceded by a Paternoster and followed by a Gloria, are recited on beads which act as counters. Five decades form a 'corona' or 'chaplet'. The first chaplet contemplates the Joyful Mysteries of the Annunciation, Visitation, Nativity, Presentation, Finding in the Temple; the second, the Sorrowful Mysteries; Agony in the Garden, Scourging, Crowning with Thorns, Carrying Cross, Crucifixion; the third, the Glorious Mysteries of the Resurrection, the Ascension, the Descent of the Spirit, the Assumption, Coronation of Virgin. The rosary was called Our Lady's Psalter or the Layfolks Psalter and formed a lay substitute for the clerical office (q.v.). The subjects familiarised by this devotion were frequently depicted and survive e.g. Adlingfleet, Yorks. (porch); Brinsop, Herefs.; Purton, Wilts.; Quenington, Glos. (tympanum); Sutton Bingham, Som.; (murals). See also s.v. each 'mystery' e.g. Annunciation.

ROYAL ARMS

Symbol of extravagant and intrusive assertion of Royal Supremacy over the Church in England at the Reformation.

Royal arms

'The curate and church-wardens of St. Martin's in Ironmonger Lane in London took down the images and pictures of the saints, and the crucifix, out of their church and painted many texts of Scripture on the walls and in the place where the crucifix was they set up the King's arms' (1547 – Burnett: History of the Reformation). The tendency to replace the symbol of Christ's death by that of the secular power as the dominant church image increased under Elizabeth I e.g. Beckington, Wilts.; Greens Norton, Northants.; Ludham, Norf. It was continued under James I, sometimes with supporting admonitions derived from his notions of sacral kingship e.g. Basingstoke, Hants.; Winsford, Som. Few examples survive from the reign of Charles I because they were an object of special hatred to the Commonwealth men who had a general addiction to iconoclasm. At the Restoration of Charles II the Royal Arms were made a compulsory item of church furniture (those at North Walsham, Norf. have the arms of the Commonwealth on the back). The Anglican Church revival of the late C19 led to the displacement or even removal of these objects.

SACRAMENT

'The sign of a sacred thing in so far as it sanctifies men' (Aquinas) i.e. the symbol 'par excellence'. Their significance is threefold:
(a) the embodiment of spiritual reality in material form is an appropriate counterpart to the union of God with man in Christ,
(b) the expression of the objectivity of God's action on the soul which is dependent not on changing subjective feeling but on obedience to

God's will,

(c) their social character as mediated through the Church – the Incarnation is extended by means of Christ's Mystical Body.

The word 'sacrament' had a very wide application in the early church but by C12 it was restricted to seven actions and the rest were regarded as 'sacramentals' (q.v.). The seven sacraments are depicted e.g. Alderford, Norf. (font); Crudwell, Wilts.; Doddiscombleigh, Devon (glass); Laxfield, Suff. (font); Melbury Bubb, Dorset (glass); Tannington, Suff.; (bench-end); Walsoken, Norf. (font); Wilby, Suff. (glass). Examples of individual sacraments as follows:

Baptism: Badingham, Suff.; Buckland, Glos.
(with Confirmation); Little Walsingham, Norf.; Nettlecombe, Som.; Thorpe Salvin, Yorks.

Penance

Confirmation: Doddiscombleigh, Devon (taking place in open air).

Eucharist: Mass – Badingham, Suff.; Brook, Marsham, Norf. Communion – Great Glemham, Suff.; Woodbridge, Suff. (with houselling cloth).

Penance: Confession – Denston, Suff.; Marsham, Norf.; Woodbridge, Suff. Scourging– Gresham, Norf.; Nettlecombe, Som.

Extreme Unction: Buckland, Glos.; Gresham, Norf.; Woodbridge, Suff.
(Communion of sick in glass at Crudwell, Wilts.; Doddiscombleigh, Devon.).

Ordination: Gresham, Norf.; Nettlecombe, Som.

Matrimony: Brook, Norf. ('care cloth' held over couple); Buckland, Glos.

SACRAMENT, BLESSED   see also *Corpus Christi*.

The Eucharist, consecrated bread (and wine) in which Christ is believed to be truly present, body, soul and Divinity. Symbolised by circular wafer (often with IHS monogram or crucifix embossed) or Host and Chalice.

Blessed sacrament
Chalice

Source of great devotion and (particularly after C12) of changes in liturgy and church furniture (aumbry, piscina, screen). The consecrated bread was kept in church at all times for veneration and for communion of the sick and dying. Its place of reservation varied: pyx, aumbry or sacrament house. The last was more

common in Scotland than in England but cf.
Milton Abbas, Dorset.

SACRAMENTALS
Objects or actions, other than sacraments (q.v.)
which have been endowed with a sacred
character by blessing, consecration or
exorcism e.g. holy water, blessed candles or
medals, church bells etc.

SACRING BELL   see *Bell, sacring.*

Aspergil and Holy
Water bucket

SACRIFICE
The central and essential religious act – the
offering of 'value' to God in recognition of its
source. That which is offered symbolises whole
creation including self. Christ's self-sacrifice
effects At-one-ment between sinful man and
perfect man and between man and God and is
the supreme symbol from which others, including
the 'effective signs' of the sacraments, draw their
power.

SAINTS   see also *Apostles; Doctors;
Evangelists.*
Martyrs were venerated by their co-religionists
from the first days of the Church and the cult
was extended to confessors by C4. At first the
practice was local and depended on local
recognition, more general recognition was
provided in the West from C10 by papal
intervention and from C12 'canonisation' (q.v.)
required papal authority. Canonisation brings
with it public recognition, authorised invocation
and church dedications, special services and
official feast day, haloed representation and the
honouring of relics (q.v.). Mediaeval devotion
led to excesses, superstition and the creation of
legendary material some of which is represented
in iconography. Saints are depicted on bosses,
brasses, misericords, screens, glass and sculpture.
Among those represented are:

Detail: martyrdom
of Thomas of
Canterbury

Agatha, V.M. C3.	Winchester cathedral (glass).	Feb. 5
Alban, protomartyr of England, C.403.	St. Alban's (brass).	Jun. 22
Aldhelm, B.C. d.709	Wiggenhall St. Mary, Norf. (glass)	May 25
Alexis, C. C5.	Tor Bryan, Wolborough, Devon. (screens).	Jul. 17

Alphege, B.M. d.1002	Greenwich, London (glass).	Apr. 19
Ambrose, B.D. d.397	Ashton, Devon (glass); Beverley minster, Yorks. (glass); Trull, Som. (pulpit).	Dec. 7
Andrew, Ap.M.	Exeter cathedral (boss).	Nov. 30
Anne, legendary mother of Virgin Mary.	Marsh Baldon, Oxon. (sculpture); Morley, Derbys. (brass); Paignton, Devon (chantry).	Jul. 26
Anthony, C.Ab. d.356	Ashton, Devon (screen); Norbury, Derbys. (glass); Plymtree, Devon; Strensham, Worcs. (screens).	Jan. 17
Apollonia, V.M. d.249	Ashton, Tor Bryan, Devon (screens).	Feb. 9
Augustine of Hippo, BCD. d.430	Ashton, Devon (screen); Trull, Som. (pulpit).	Aug. 28
Barbara, V.M. d.c. 306?	Bawburgh, Norf. (glass); Carlisle Deanery (boss); Norwich St. Peter Mancroft (alabaster); Ranworth, Norf.; Whimple, Devon (screens).	Dec. 4
Bartholomew, Ap.M.	Blythburgh, Suff. (carving); Hereford cathedral chantry (carving); Lostwithiel, Cornw. (alabaster).	Aug. 24
Blaise, B.M. d.316?	Exeter St. Mary Steps (screen); Oxford Christchurch (glass).	Feb. 3
Botolph, Ab.C. d.c.700	Wiggenhall St. Mary, Norf. (glass).	Jun. 17
Bidget of Sweden, Q. mystic: d.1373	Westhall, Suff.; Wolborough, Devon, (screens).	Jul. 23
Catherine of Alexandria, V.M. d.310?	Beverley minster, Yorks. (tomb sculpt,); Combe-in-Teignhead, Cornw.. (bench-end); Deerhurst, Glos. (glass); Ludlow, Salop. (glass); Norwich St. Helen's hospital (boss); Patrington, Yorks. (boss); Plymtree, Devon (screen); Selworthy, Devon (boss); West Wickham, Kent (glass); Widecombe, Devon (boss).	Nov. 25
Catherine of Siena, V. d.1380	Portlemouth, Tor Bryan, Wolborough Devon (screens).	Apr. 30
Cecilia, V.M. C2.	Kenton, Devon (screen).	Nov. 22
Christopher, C.M. d.250?	Morley, Derbys. (brass); Selworthy, Som. (boss); Shapwick, Dorset (bell); Terrington St. Clement, Norf. (mural); York All Saints (glass).	Jul. 25
Clement, P.M. d.c.100	Ashton, Whimple, Devon (screens).	Nov. 23
Cosmas and Damian MM. c.290.	Wolborough, Devon (screen).	Sep. 27
Cuthbert, B.C. d.687	Durham cathedral (sculpture); Methley, Yorks. (glass); Westminster Henry VII chapel (sculpture).	Mar. 20
Denis, B.M. d.95?	Alphington, Cheriton Bishop, Devon; Grafton Regis, Northants. (screens); Methley, Yorks. (glass).	Oct. 9

Dorothy, V.M. d.287?	Ashton, Plymtree, Devon (screens).	Feb. 6
Dunstan, B.C. d.988	Great Plumstead, Norf. (mural); Ludlow, Salop.; Oxford Bodleian library (glass).	May 19
Edmund, K.M. d.870	Bristol cathedral Lady chapel (glass); Ely cathedral (stall); Pulham St. Mary, Norf. (porch); Tewkesbury, Glos. (boss).	Nov. 20
Edward, K.M. d.978	Alphington, Devon (screen); Exeter West front (sculpture); Wells cathedral West front (sculpture).	Mar. 18
Edward, K.C. d.1066	Malvern, Worcs. (glass); Norwich cathedral cloisters (boss); Wells cathedral; Westminster (sculptures).	Oct. 13
Elizabeth C. C1. Mother of John Baptist	Morley, Derbys. (glass).	Nov. 5
Elizabeth of Hungary, Q.C. d.1231	Ludlow, Salop. (glass); Westminster Henry VII chapel (sculpture) – ?	Nov. 19
Eloy, B.C. d.c.660	Durweston, Dorset (sculpture); Fakenham, Suff. (sculpture); Ugborough, Devon (boss).	Dec. 1
Erasmus, B.M. d.305?	Hennock, Devon|; Lullingstone, Kent; Sandringham, Norf. (screens); Westminster Henry VII chapel (sculpture).	Jun. 2
Ethelbert, K.M. d.793	Hereford, Wells cathedrals (sculptures).	May 20
Etheldreda, Q.Ab. d.679	Ely cathedral, (bosses); Ranworth, Norf.; Wolborough, Devon (screens).	Jun. 23
Faith, V.M. d.303	Norwich St. Lawrence (brass); Westminster Abbey chapel (mural).	Oct. 6
Francis of Assisi, C. d.1226	Alphington, Bradninch, Devon; Hempstead, Stalham, Norf. (screens).	Oct. 4
Frideswide, V.C. C8.	Oxford Christchurch (bosses).	Oct. 19
Gabriel, archangel	Gresford, Denbighs. (glass); Warkworth, Northants. (bench-end).	
Genevieve, V.C. d.512	Kenn, Devon (screen).	Jan. 3
George, M. C4	Banwell, Som. (bosses); Elsing, Norf. (brass); Pickering, Yorks. (mural); St. Neot, Cornw. (glass); Wootton Courtney, Som.; Worcester St. Andrew (bosses).	Apr. 23
Giles, C.Ab. Hermit C7	Bradninch, Devon; Great Plumstead, Norf. (murals); Sandringham, Wiggenhall St. Mary, Norf. (glass).	Sep. 1
Gregory, P.D. d.605	Macclesfield, Ches. (brass); Paignton, Devon (sculpture); Trull, Som. (pulpit).	Mar. 12
Helen, C. Empress d.328	Alphington, Devon (screen); Ashton-u-Lyne, Lancs. (glass); Morley, Derbys.	Aug. 18

	(glass); Norwich St. Peter Mancroft (alabaster); Tor Bryan, Devon (screen).	
Hubert, B.C. d.727	Kenn, Devon (screen).	Nov. 3
Isidore, C. d.c.400?	Curry Rivel, Som. (glass).	Jan. 15
Jerome, C.D. d.420	Ashton, Devon (screen); Oxford All Souls (glass); Trull, Som. (pulpit).	Sep. 30
John Baptist, C.M. C1	Apsley Guise, Beds. (brass); Ottery St. Mary, Devon; Patrington, Yorks. (bosses); Plymtree, Devon (screen); York All Saints (glass).	Jun. 24
John Evangelist, Ap. C1	Lincoln cathedral (glass); Westminster Abbey (sculpture); York All Saints (glass).	Dec. 27
John of Beverley, B.C. d.721	Beverley St. Mary, Yorks. (boss); Hexham, Northd. (sculpture); Wells cathedral Lady chapel (glass).	May 7
John of Bridlington, C. d.1379	Morley, Derbys. (glass).	Oct. 9
Julian of Le Mans, B. C3?	Kenn, Devon (screen).	Jan. 27
Julian Hospitaller, C. Hermit, C4?	Wiggenhall St. Mary Magdalene, Norf. (glass).	Jan. 9
Lambert, B.M. d.709	Shrewsbury St. Mary (glass).	Sep. 17
Lawrence, M. d.258	Abbots Langley, Herts. (mural); Ludlow, Salop. (glass); Nettlestead, Kent (glass); Norwich cathedral cloisters (boss); Ranworth, Norf. (screen); Westminster St. Mary crypt (boss).	Aug. 10
Leger, B.M. d.678	Ashton, Devon (screen).	Oct. 2
Leonard, C. d.c.559	Durham cathedral chapter house; Sandringham, Norf. (glass).	Nov. 6
Lucy, V.M. d.304	Kenton, Devon (screen).	Dec. 13
Margaret of Antioch V.M. C4?	Norwich St. Peter Mancroft (alabaster); Plymtree, Devon; Ranworth, Norf. (screens); Sherborne, Dorset. (misericord); Westminster St. Mary crypt (boss).	Jul. 20
Martha, V. C1 (Luke 10.38ff.)	Westminster Henry VII chapel (sculpture).	Jul. 29
Martin of Tours, B.C. d.397	Beverley minster, Yorks. (glass); Great Plumstead, Norf. (mural); Lincoln cathedral tower (boss); Norwich cathedral cloister (boss); Shrewsbury St. Mary, Salop.; York St. Martin (glass).	Nov. 11
Mary Cleopas, C. C1 (John 19.25)	York Holy Trinity Goodramgate (glass).	Apr. 9
Mary Magdalene, C. C1	Combe-in-Teignhead, Devon (bench-end); Lincoln cathedral (misericord);	Jul. 22

	Norwich cathedral (bosses).	
Nicholas of Myra, B.C. C4	Beverley minster, Yorks.; Hillesden, Bucks.; Malvern, Worcs. (glass); Norwich cathedral cloisters (boss).	Dec. 6
Olave, K.M. d.1030	Barton Turf Norf.; Wolborough, Devon (screens); York St. Olave (external sculpture).	Jul. 29
Osyth, Q.M.Ab. d.653?	Long Melford, Suff. (glass).	Oct. 7
Pancras M. d.304	Cowfold, Sussex (brass)	May 12
Paul, Ap.M. C1	Exeter cathedral St. Paul's chapel (boss); Lincoln cathedral (glass); Ranworth, Norf. (screen).	Jun. 30
Paulinus, B.C. d.644	Methley, Yorks.; York minster (glass).	Oct. 10
Petronilla, V. C1	North Elmham, Norf., Wolborough, Devon (screens).	May 31
Roche, C. d.1337	Hennock, Holne, Kenn, Plymtree, Whimple, Devon (screens).	Aug. 16
Sebastian, M. 288	Bradninch, Ugborough, Devon (screens).	Jan. 20
Sidwell, V.M. d.c.700?	Exeter St. Sidwell (sculpture); Plymtree Devon (screen and eight others in county).	Aug. 1
Sitha, V.C. (Zita) d.1271	Ashton, Devon; Barton Turf. Norf. (screens); Plymtree, Devon (screen); Mells, Som. (glass); North Elmham, Norf. (screen).	Apr. 27
Stephen, first martyr (Acts 7.56ff.)	Paignton, Devon (glass).	Dec. 26
Swithun, B.C. d.862	Wiggenhall St. Mary Magdalene, Norf. (glass).	Jul. 2
Thomas of Canterbury, B.M. d.1170	Cowfold, Sussex (brass); Exeter cathedral; Ottery St. Mary, Devon (bosses); Plymtree, Devon (screen).	Dec. 29
Thomas of Hereford, B.C. d.1287	Ross-on-Wye, Herefs. (glass).	Oct. 2
Ursula, V.M. C5?	Ashton, Devon (screen); Hucknall, Morley, Derbys.; York Holy Trinity Goodramgate (glass).	Oct. 21
Valentine, M. d.c.270?	'Valentines' are not related to saint but to pre-Christian practices on this day.	Feb. 14
Victor, M. d.303?	Tor Bryan, Devon (screen).	Jul. 21
Vincent, M. d.304	Curry Rivel, Som.; Payhembury, Devon (glass).	Jan. 22
Wilfrid, B.C. d.709	Ripon cathedral, Yorks. (alabaster).	Oct. 12
Wilgefortis, V.M. (Uncumber)	mythical, due to misinterpretation of early crucifix. Westminster, Henry VII chapel (sculpture).	Jul. 20
William of York, B.C. d.1154	Morley, Derbys. (glass); Wolborough, Devon (screen); York All Saints, York minster (glass).	Jun. 8

| Winifred, V.M. d.c.600 | Balsham, Cambs. (brass); Westminster Henry VII chapel (sculpture). | Nov. 3 |
| Wulstan, B.C. d.1095 | Malvern, Worcs. (glass). | Jun. 7 |

Abbreviations:
   Ab.abbot or abbess, Ap.Apostle, B.bishop or archbishop, C.confessor (saintly life without martyrdom), D.doctor (q.v.), E.one of four Gospel-writers (evangelist), K.king, M.martyr, P.pope, Q.queen, V.virgin of holy life. d.died, c.about (circa).

Arms of St. Edmund

Iconography provides interesting examples of public veneration before official canonisation e.g. Henry VI, whose cause was initiated but not completed, appears on screens at Barton Turf, Gately, Norf.; Whimple, Devon.; alongside (in the first two cases) John Schorne (d.1308), a saintly parish priest who is also represented at Alphington, Devon; Binham Abbey, Gately, Litcham, Ludham, Norf.; Portleborough, Wolborough, Devon.

SANCTUARY

1. Holy place, presbytery, easternmost part of chancel containing altar.

2. Place of refuge. In Middle Ages a criminal could take refuge in a church for 40 days during which time he could abjure the country and be given safe-conduct to an appointed port. Those claiming this privilege had sometimes to grasp a particular object, originally the altar. See Fridstool, Knocker.

SARACEN'S HEAD

After Crusades, Saracen became sterotype of 'rejector of Christ' and such characters were represented as Saracens e.g. Coventry Holy Trinity, Warks. (misericord); Malvern, Worcs. (glass); Stratford, Warks. (misericord).

SATIRE

Satire: geese hanging fox

There is a strong satirical element in mediaeval art and literature: irreverent images of the upper classes, clerical and lay; grotesques and gargoyles; representations of arrogance, foolishness and proverbial saws. There are images of friars as foxes and their hearers as geese, mockery of women's foibles and upper-class sports and attitudes and a liking for 'topsy-turveydom'.

Scales

SCALES
Symbol of equity and of Divine Justice.
Sometimes an attribute of St. Michael (q.v.) who
weighed souls in scales. The angelic order (q.v.)
of Thrones sometimes bears scales. They also
appear in representations of 'Christ of the Trades'
(q.v.) where they are a warning against inequitable
labour: under-working or under-paid.

SCRIPTURE   see also *Types*.
The mediaevals, following traditional practice,
interpreted Scripture in four ways or senses:
   Historical (literal) as narration of events,
   Allegorical as saying one thing but meaning
      another (an earthly metaphor),
   Tropological (moral) as applied to
      contemporary behaviour,
   Anagogical as moving from visible to invisible
      (a heavenly metaphor).
Thus a text concerning Jesus could be taken as
referring to the historical person in his earthly
body, as a reference to his 'mystical' body (the
Church), as exemplary for our own behaviour or
as a metaphor of the way the life of Christ shows
us the way to glory. 'Jerusalem is understood
historically of that earthly city whither pilgrims
journey; allegorically, of the Church Militant;
tropologically, of every faithful soul; anagogically,
of the celestial Jerusalem which is our country.'
(Durandus). These four senses have to be borne
in mind when interpreting Scriptural figures and
we must remember that the 'spiritual sense' of
Scripture did not represent a personal or private
symbolism but was a hallowed tradition
authorised by the Bible itself e.g. New Adam,
serpent in wilderness, Paschal lamb.

Choir seat or stall

SEATS   see also *Pews*.
Originally little provision for laity except at base
of pillars and along nave wall (e.g. Campsall,
Yorks.) hence 'the weak to the wall'. When not
standing or kneeling the congregation sat on the
rush-strewn floor (the wealthy brought their own
cushions). When seating was provided the bench-
ends (q.v.) provided location for decoration and
edification e.g. Blythburgh, Suff.; Dunton
Bassett, Leics.; Finedon, Northants.; Kilkhampton,
Cornw.; Trull, Som.; Winthorpe, Lincs.

Sedilia

SEDILIA
Elaborate (stone) seats on South side of chancel for Mass ministers: priest, deacon and sub-deacon. Often associated with piscina (q.v.) e.g. Chaddesley Corbett, Worcs.; Chesterton, Oxon.; Filey, Yorks.; Grafton Underwood, Northants.; Malpas, Ches.; Rotherham, Yorks.; Tideswell, Derbys.; Uffington, Berks. Other numbers than three seats occur: two (for priest and clerk); four (for three ministers and clerk); five (for ministers and two clerks). Rare example of wooden sedilia at Hexham, Northd.

SEVEN CORPORAL WORKS   see *Corporal Works.*

SEVEN DEADLY SINS   see *Sins, Seven Deadly.*

SEVEN GIFTS OF HOLY SPIRIT
Wisdom, Knowledge, Counsel, Fortitude, Learning, Piety, Godly Fear.

SEVEN SACRAMENTS   see also *Sacraments.*
'Seven Sacrament' fonts are frequent in East Anglia e.g. Badingham, Cratfield, Suff.; Gresham, Sloley, Norf. Original colour is discernible at Great Witchingham, Norf.; Westhall, Suff. Of thirty-three such fonts, only two (Farningham, Kent; Nettlecombe, Som.) lie outside East Anglia.

SHEILA-NA-GIG
Grotesque female fertility symbol e.g. Austerfield, Yorks. (capital); Bristol St. Mary Redcliffe (boss); Kilpeck, Herefs. (corbel); South Tawton, Devon. (boss); Whittlesford, Cambs. (tower).

SHIP   see also *Ark.*
A 'natural' symbol of precarious security in encompassing danger, of progress towards a goal, of adventure between two points of rest and having this content in both Jewish and Greek (Odyssey) thought. The Christians noticed that its mast and transverse yard form a cross and its anchor is a symbol of hope, so it became a symbol of the Church. Sometimes takes the form of an ark (see Type) and it may be beset by sirens (see Fabulous Beasts) e.g. Brook, Kent (mural); Winchester cathedral

Ship

(font).

It may be naturalistic and refer to occupation e.g. Bishops Lydeard, Som.; East Budleigh, Devon (bench-ends); Thaxted, Essex (glass); Tiverton, Devon (bench-end etc.). There are scratch drawings of ships on walls and pillars of coastal churches e.g. Blakeney, Cley, Norf.; Margaret-at-Cliffe, Kent; Newbourn, Suff.; Salthouse, Norf.; Welbourn, Lincs.; Wiveton, Norf.

SHRINE

Shrine

If churches did not originate in a shrine they often tried to acquire an object for enshrinement to increase their status (and income). St. Lawrence, Evesham was built for pilgrims to the tomb of Simon de Montfort; the porch at Grantham for devotees of St. Wulfram. There is a small chapel to Richard de Wyche, a local saint, in Droitwich St. Andrew, Worcs. Whitchurch Canonicorum, Dorset still has the shrine of St. Wite with the characteristic apertures to allow a near approach to the venerated body. Westminster possesses the royal shrine of Edward the Confessor and there are remains of a humbler shrine at St. Endellion, Cornw. There were shrines to Thomas at Canterbury, Werburgh at Chester, Cuthbert at Durham, Etheldreda (Audrey) at Ely (hence 'tawdry'), Cantelupe at Hereford, Frideswide at Oxford etc.

SHROVETIDE

First week of Lent. Shrove Tuesday was last opportunity for 'shrift' (confession and absolution) as a proper beginning to Lent. People working after this day were bumped on the 'Bradley stone' in church yard of Norton-in-Hales, Salop. The 'pancake-bell' at Olney, Bucks., was earlier called the 'shriving-bell'. Pancakes were part of a celebration, carnival (carni-vale, farewell to the flesh).

SINS, SEVEN DEADLY   see also *Virtues and Vices.*

Pride, covetousness, lust, envy, gluttony, anger, sloth. Pride was the chief but all were 'principles' in that they each included a number of other failings. Gluttony included drinking to excess, lust included any inordinate desire, anger

Son of God emblems

included strife and suicide and sloth extended to spiritual, as well as physical, laziness. They were often placed in antithesis to the Corporal Works of Mercy (q.v.) or the Seven Gifts of the Spirit (q.v.) e.g. Broughton, Bucks.; Corby, Lincs. (murals); Thornham, Norf. (bench-end); Trotton, Sussex (mural); Warmington, Northants. (corbel).

SON OF GOD   see also *Christ; Doom; Majestas.*
The second Person of the Trinity (q.v.) who is symbolised by Alpha and Omega, Cross, Vine etc. but especially by the Agnus Dei (q.v.). The content of this emblem is mainly derived from Revelation where it occurs twenty-nine times, recapitulating dozens of Old Testament references and associations in the light of the New Testament fulfilment. The themes are sacrifice, atonement, union of mankind with God, priesthood, Temple, Incarnation, Resurrection, Ascension, Glory.

SOUL
Often represented as a small, naked figure: weighed in the scales of St. Michael, standing before St. Peter, clutched in the claws of the devil or safe in Abraham's bosom (e.g. Beverley minster Percy tomb, Yorks.).

It may be portrayed symbolically as a dove or rabbit or as the prey of bird or beast. e.g. Balsham, Cambs.; Checkendon, Oxon. (brass); Derby All Saints (tomb-stone); York All Saints (roof).

SPADE   see also *Labours of the Months.*
Attribute of Christ in Resurrection appearance to Mary Magdalene (John 20.11–18) e.g. Canterbury cathedral water-tower (glass); Lincoln cathedral (misericord); Yaxley, Hunts. (mural). It is also an attribute of Adam after the Expulsion. Symbol of drudgery consequent upon the Fall (q.v.), of the Good Work wrought by Christ and of the redemption of labour.

SPANDREL
The roughly triangular space between the curve of an arch and the enclosing right angle which was sometimes filled by symbolic designs e.g. angel choir, Lincoln.

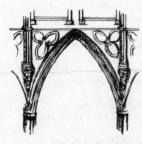

Spandrel

SPEAKING IN CHURCH   see also *Jangling; Tutivillius.*

Properly, prayer, praise and thanksgiving through Psalms, Hymns, Spiritual Songs combined in the Liturgy. It is not the place for secular conversation: 'We must abstain from superfluous and irreverent words because it is the palace of the King of kings and filled with angels.' (Durandus). Distraction was to be avoided during the words of the service which were to be treated with the utmost respect as a sacramental (q.v.).

SPIRE

The pointed termination of a church tower which was far commoner in the Middle Ages than today due to destruction and collapse through disrepair. Almost all towers seem to have been intended to have a spire. Usually seen as a finger pointing to heaven though some moderns see it as a phallic symbol. Durandus says that it 'signifieth how perfectly and inviolably the Catholic Faith must be held; "which Faith except a man do keep whole and undefiled, without doubt he shall perish everlastingly" (Athanasian Creed)'. Perhaps it was some intimation of this which produced George Fox's hatred of 'steeple houses'! e.g. Chesterfield, Derbys.; Louth, Lincs. and for the common wooden spires of the South-East where stone is scarce: Compton, Surrey.

Spires

SQUINT

Narrow, oblique opening cut through wall to afford view of altar. Its purpose was
(a) to allow a priest celebrating at a minor altar to observe the mass at the High Altar so that he would not begin his own before the Elevation
(b) to open up the view of the Elevation generally as this was the moment for adoration, spiritual communion etc. (Elevation: raising of the host and chalice above the celebrant's head immediately after the consecration). e.g. Bridgewater, Som.; Gloucester St. Nicholas; Lewes, Sussex; Newnham Murren, Oxon.; North Cerney, Northleach, Glos.; Quatt, Salop.; Scawton, Yorks.; Warkworth hermitage, Northd.; West Tanfield, Yorks.

Squint

    Some squints may have been for security: to allow guardian in tower-chamber or elsewhere

Squint

Stained glass window

to watch reliquary or other treasure. Others may have been for the benefit of the sacring-bell ringer e.g. Durham St. Oswald.

STAINED GLASS

There are insignificant survivals of Romanesque work but rather more early Gothic (C13), usually consisting of figures in deep-toned medallions (often united by Jesse-tree (q.v.)) or of pale grisaille diapering e.g. Chetwode, Bucks.; Westwell, Kent. In middle Gothic (C14) the artificial medallions were superseded by more realistic figures, canopied as in contemporary stonework, and the colour-range is extended e.g. Aldwinckle, Stanford-on-Avon, Northants. The C15 introduced 'silver stain' which produced brilliant and rich colours, often exploited in heraldry e.g. Almondbury, Yorks.; St. Neot, Cornw.; Winscombe, Som. Renaissance glass is occasionally found e.g. Cambridge King's College chapel and there is much Victorian work (some of high quality e.g. Baldersby, Nun Monkton, Yorks.) and, more rarely, good modern work e.g. Tudeley, Kent. The finest examples of mediaeval work, both in quantity and quality, are in the churches of York but Fairford, Glos. and Ludlow St. Lawrence, Salop. are also outstanding.

STALLS

Convents and collegiate churches provided elaborate choir seating for their ministers, often with rich canopies and carved misericords (q.v.) The number of stalls may be taken as an indication of the size of the community. The carved projection on the sides of a stall ('elbow') is often carved e.g. Nantwich, Ches.; Southwold, Suff. Surviving mediaeval stalls in parish churches include: Barkstone, Leics.; Boston, Lincs.; Gresford, Denbighs.; Hemingborough, Yorks.; Hull Holy Trinity, Yorks.; Ivychurch, Kent; Lancaster (from priory); Ludham, Norf.; Nantwich, Ches.; Thanet, Kent; Winthorpe, Lincs. The remains from the great chantry at Fotheringhay are scattered in neighbouring churches: Benefield, Hemington, Tansor, Northants.

Station of the cross

STATIONS OF THE CROSS

A series of paintings or carvings depicting incidents of Good Friday. They arose as a substitute for the devout following of the Way of the Cross in Jerusalem and were popularised by the Franciscans in the late Middle Ages. In their modern form they offer fourteen incidents for prayer and meditation: Christ is condemned to death, receives the cross, falls, meets His mother, is helped by Simon, has His face wiped by Veronica, falls again, meets the women of Jerusalem, falls a third time, is stripped naked, nailed to the cross, dies, His body is taken down, and laid in the sepulchre.

STIGMATA

On Sept. 15, 1224, St. Francis had a mystical experience after which his own body reproduced the five wounds of Christ (stigmata) depicted e.g. on screens at Bradninch, Devon; Hempstead, Norf.; Kenn, Devon; Stalham, Norf.

STONES AND MINERALS

Have symbolic significance e.g.

Carbuncle: blood, suffering, Christ's Passion, martyrdom.

Chalcedony: holiness.

Coral: protection against the 'evil eye'.

Gold: (*a*) the heavenly realm (*b*) mammon, wordly wealth, idolatry.

Ivory: purity, strength, incorruptibility (hence use in crucifix figure).

Jasper: faith.

Rock: solid foundation, Christ, Peter.

Salt: pervasive strength, incorruptibility.

Silver: purity, chastity, eloquence.

Stones: firmness. Attribute of Alphege, Stephen.

Water: cleansing, purifying, innocence (see Baptism, Water). Water mixed with wine in Eucharistic chalice symbolises assumption of humanity into Divinity. A fountain or spring may symbolise Paradise, sacraments, Virgin Mary.

STOUP

Basin for holy water at church entrance. 'Wherefore he that entereth into a church

Stoup

fortifieth himself with the sign of the cross' (Durandus). Three fingers (in honour of the Trinity) are dipped into the water with which the sign of the cross is made from the forehead, over the chest and left to right shoulder symbolising the consecration of the whole person in thought, word and deed, in mind, body and spirit. A symbolic washing before entering church as a sign 'of the purity of soul with which the Throne of Majesty should be approached' is as old as the Christian church.

The stoup is usually on the right of the entrance but there is a left-handed one at Crowle, Worcs. and one on either side at East Dereham, Norf.; Irthingborough, Northants. Right-handed stoups at e.g. Auckland St. Helen, Durham (converted Roman altar); Broughton Astley, Leics.; Caldecote, Herts.; Endellion, Cornw.; Harlton St. Mary, Cambs.; Lastingham, Yorks.; Moresby, Cumb. (now font); Pylle, Som.; Thorpe-by-Newark, Notts. (now font); Wootton Courtney, Som.

SUN DIAL   see *Dial; Time*.

SWASTIKA
Also known as fylfot, occurs in Troy, India and China as well as in Christian decoration. It seems to have been a sun and light symbol, and the form which 'rotates' anti-clockwise (e.g. Nazi) represents evil and darkness e.g. Chartham, Kent (brass); Hathersage, Derbys.; Mexborough, Yorks. (bells); Nevern, Pembr. (obelisks).

Swastika (Fylfot)

SWORD
Attribute of martyrs slain by this instrument, particularly of St. Paul. 'The sword denotes the ire of Saul; the book the power converting Paul'. It can also, when pointed upwards, symbolise the 'sword of the Spirit' (Ephes. 6.17).

Sword

SYBIL
The sybils were prophetesses of the classical world who were seen as analogous to the Jewish prophets with whom they are often associated in iconography. There are usually twelve depicted e.g. Bradninch, Heavitree, Ugborough, Devon (screens).

Scallop shell

Flower Symbols

Table tomb

SYMBOLS

Prior to words and beyond them since they allow conception, recall and consideration without experience or encounter. They are open-ended and convey instantly what would require a multitude of words if it could be expressed verbally at all. They are particularly apposite instruments for the communication of moral and theological ideas because they imitate the reality of these areas by the multiplicity of their significance and relationships. Whereas description abstracts from reality, symbolism presents it by an immediate message accompanied by an ever-widening web of associations. Their use implies a belief in the integrity of all things, the total meaningfulness of creation, and the consonance of all its uncorrupted parts. It is not insignificant that the old word for 'Creed' is 'Symbol'.

TABLE   see *Altar; Communion Table, Credence.*
For tables of Commandments, Lord's Prayer, Creed see Creed.

TABLE TOMB
Originated inside church where they doubled as chantry altars or Easter sepulchres. Occasionally found in church yard (ejected?) e.g. Bishopstone, Wilts.; Eccleston, Lancs.; Kellington, Yorks.; Loversall, Yorks. A decadent form was revived in C18-19.

TE DEUM
A C4 Latin hymn to the Father and Son, attributed to Ambrose and Augustine, sung solemnly as a formal corporate act of thanksgiving.

TEMPLE CHURCH
Church formerly belonging to Knights Templar, a military order founded in 1118 to defend the Holy Places in Palestine. They were built in a round form in imitation of the church of the Holy Sepulchre e.g. London Strand. Other churches with round naves: Cambridge; Little Maplestead, Essex; Northampton.

THREE LIVING AND THREE DEAD   see
also *Memento Mori*.

A C13 French poem describes how three
hunting gallants encounter three corpses who
give three warnings: 'Thus will ye be and as ye
are so once were we', 'Rich must die as well as
poor', 'None may escape', e.g. Charlwood,
Surrey; Peakirk, Northants.; Widford, Oxon. The
same theme lies behind 'Death and the Maiden'
and 'Death and the Gallant' (Newark, Notts.
chantry) and underlines the inscription on the
Black Prince's tomb (Canterbury cathedral) and
the development of the 'contrast' tomb with the
deceased in splendid robes above and a rotting
cadaver beneath. A late brass at Hunsdon, Herts.
shows Death striking both huntsman and his
quarry.

THRONE   see *Angelic Orders; Chair*.

TIARA

Triple papal crown, dating from 1315, allegedly
symbolising the three-fold spiritual power of
teaching, ruling, sanctifying or triple office of
prophet, pastor and priest. Found in late
representations of God the Father.

TILE

Encaustic tiles often bear symbolic motifs and
there is evidence that symbolism once extended
to the floor, especially in larger churches (see
Labyrinth). Individual tiles survive at Acton
Burnell, Salop.; Bosgrove, Etchingham, Sussex;
Gloucester Cathedral; Jervaulx Abbey, Yorks.;
Lewes Priory, Sussex; Malvern, Worcs.;
Muchelney, Som.; Somerton, Oxon.; West
Hendred, Berks.

Tiles

TIME

The church is the meeting place of time and
eternity and both were symbolically represented:
eternity in the general decoration of the quire
and time in the Labours of the Months, Signs of
the Zodiac etc. Great churches had mechanical
clocks often with symbolic ornament and sundials
were frequent (the later ones often having a moral
inscription). Sundials at e.g. Daglingworth, Glos.;
Kirkdale, Weaverthorpe, Yorks.

TOMBS AND MEMORIALS   see also *Brass; Hog-back; Shrine; Table Tomb.*

Mediaeval survivals are of knights, prelates and patrons. Knights are indicated by an incised sword (see Coffins) or armoured recumbent effigy. Crossed legs (e.g. Dorchester, Oxon.; Whatton, Notts.) do not necessarily imply a crusader. The pomp and splendour of estate is often contrasted with the levelling of death, especially in the case of prelates e.g. Exeter, Lincoln, Wells cathedrals. There is a fine lay example at Ewelme, Oxon. and a continuance of the convention at Hatfield, Herts. Poignant human touches occur e.g. Lowick, Northants. where lord and his lady are still handfast in death (specified in contract for monument); Bodenham, Herefs. has child sheltering in folds of lady's dress and at Elford, Staffs. a boy holds the tennis-ball which accidentally killed him. Mediaeval tombs may be found in graveyards e.g. Saxton, Yorks. and tomb-chests often have rich detail e.g. Chillingham, Northd.; Harewood, Yorks.; Ross-on-Wye, Herefs.; Skipton, Yorks.; Willoughby-in-the-Wolds, Notts.

Tomb

TOOLS   see also *Trades, Christ of.*

Occur as attributes or emblems e.g. Club, bat – James the Less; Compasses (q.v.); Comb (iron) – Blaise; Gridiron – Lawrence; Hammer – Instrument of Passion (q.v.); Hatchet, axe – Matthew, Matthias; Knife (flaying) – Bartholomew; Lance – Jude, Thomas, instrument of Passion; pen – doctors, evangelists; pincers – Agatha, Apollonia, instruments of Passion; plane – Thomas, Joseph (in some modern representations); saw – Simon Zelotes; set-square or builders rule – Thomas.

TOWER   see also *Spire.*

Not consecrated, as strictly it is not part of the church and may be actually detached e.g. Evesham, Worcs.; West Walton, Norf. Open to symbolism: the spire pointing by day, the lantern gleaming at night, the bells calling day and night made it both a material and spiritual guide to the wayfarer. Nevertheless it served very practical purposes of which the prime one was to house bells e.g. Ormskirk, Lancs. It was a

Tower

Tracery

refuge from floods and stronghold in times of tumult (church-towers on Scottish border doubled as 'pele' towers e.g. Great Salkeld, Cumb.), hence its battlements and protected entrance. It could provide a mark for seafarers e.g. Blakeney, Norf. or a light for other travellers (Weldon, Northants.; York All Saints Pavement). Often it provided accommodation: for a priest, a hermit, a 'watcher' (over reliquary, q.v.) or even a small school.

TRACERY
The stonework to support glass within a large window aperture. Durandus saw even this as symbolical: windows of two lights indicating the two precepts of charity (Matthew. 22.37–40) or the missionary activity of the church as the apostles went out two by two. Other have seen two lights as symbolising the two Natures of Christ, three the Trinity etc. (see Numbers). In some instances the tracery itself is undoubtedly symbolic e.g. Jesse windows (q.v.); York minster West window.

TRADES, CHRIST OF
In widely separated areas of England (e.g. Breage, Cornw.; Michaelchurch Escley, Herefs.; Oaksey, Wilts.) there is evidence of a figure of Christ standing, usually with up-raised arms, surrounded by tools and showing His wounds. These are taken to symbolise the sanctity of labour (Christ was a carpenter who wrought the world's redemption in the wood of the Tree) and also His wounding by sacrilegious or slovenly work. The figure at Fingringhoe, Essex bears the inscription 'In omnia opere memento finis' which would appear to mean 'In all you do bear in mind its purpose and your end'. The surrounding 'tools' sometimes include recreational objects. The Middle Ages sometimes spoke of honest craftsmen as 'Goddes knyghtes' and referred to Christ as 'chief of all craftsmen and source of all the arts in the world'. At Ampney St. Mary, Glos. and Stedham, Sussex, the Christ of Trades balances the representation of St. George, patron of the knightly class. Perhaps the symbolism is related to Ecclesiasticus 38.31ff.: 'All these put their trust in their hands. . .they will maintain

the fabric of the world and in the handiwork of their craft is their prayer'.

Trade

TRADE, PROFESSION
Masons and carpenters are represented at e.g. Beverley St. Mary, Yorks.; Brampton, Derbys.; Christchurch, Hants.; Great Doddington, Northants., a shoemaker at Wellingborough, Northants., and a sexton at Ludlow, Salop., while a fuller with all his tools appears at Spaxton, Som. (bench-ends). Trade symbols on coffin-lids (q.v.) again became popular in C18 and appear on tomb-stones e.g. Blakeney, Norf. (mariner); East Grinstead, Sussex (schoolmaster); Lewes St. John, Sussex (carpenter); Maresfield, Sussex (roadman); Painswick, Glos.; Saffron Walden, Essex (freemasons).

TRANSEPTS
Though sometimes given symbolic significance as providing the 'arms' of a cruciform church, transepts seem to have arisen as one answer to the purely practical problem of providing space for additional altars associated with guilds, chantries or special devotions e.g. Chartham, Kent; Heckington, Lincs.; Paignton, Devon; Patrington, Yorks.; Witney, Oxon.

TREE OF LIFE   see also *Flowers. . .; Garden.*
Sometimes is a metamorphosis of Norse Yggdrasil (q.v.) in the same way that Odin's fight with the Hell-worm changes to Michael and the Dragon e.g. Dinton, Bucks., but the fundamental source of this imagery is the Bible: the Tree of Paradise and the Tree of the Cross e.g. Kilpeck, Herefs. (South door). The tree was a popular symbol e.g. tree of Jesse, Christ as the Tree of virtue with the corporal works of mercy as His fruits. There was an analogous tree of Death which bore the Seven Deadly Sins (q.v.). Trees appear at e.g. Abingdon, Berks.; Chalfont St. Giles, Bucks.; Chalgrove, Oxon.; Godshill, I o. W. (murals); Lower Swell, Glos.; Siston, Glos.; Stratton, Glos.; Stoke sub Hamdon, Som.; Weston Longville, Norf. (tympana).

Tree

TREE, SACRED   see also *Jack o' the Green; Yggdrasil; Yew.*

Trees were a common object of pre-Christian worship and some people have found a reminiscence of the sacred grove in the piers and vaulting of great churches. Tree cults (of which the Yule-log is a survival) took two forms (both of which were fertility rites):

(a) Worship of the tree personalised through sacred round-dance (cf. Maypole),

(b) 'Arborisation' of human being by masking him/her in foliage with an associated solemn procession.

Jack o' the Green is related to the second while survivals of the first may include the dance round the church at Painswick, Glos., the wassailing of the apple-tree at Carhampton, Som., and oak trees with a title e.g. Gospel Oak, Polstead, Suff.; Major Oak, Sherwood, Notts.

TRINITY, HOLY

The representation of a Tri-Une God presents obvious difficulties in spite of the tendency to see it adumbrated in any three-fold item or triple division within the church: nave, chancel, sanctuary; three towers or spires; the triforium arcade; a triple order of moulding on an arch; three altar steps; three fingers of blessing; trefoil; equilateral triangle. Some of these items are more likely symbols than others but none may be dismissed out of hand e.g. a boss at Stamford St. Mary, Lincs. has a face with an equilateral triangle in its mouth – 'preaching the Trinity'? There are corbels and bosses in which three fishes form a triangle – 'Christ is God, God is Triune, God is Spirit'? e.g. Stanground, Hunts. (poppy head).

Holy Trinity

Other attempts took an anthropological form: a tricephalic head or three identical figures e.g. Bristol St. Mary Recliffe, (boss); Cartmel, Lancs. (misericord); Lansallos, Cornw. (bench-end); Norwich cathedral nave (boss); Peterborough cathedral choir, (boss); Windsor St. George, Berks.; Worcester cathedral cloisters (bosses). These forms were repugnant aesthetically and theologically (tending towards tritheism) and were replaced by representations of an old man (Ancient of Days) holding a crucifix with an associated dove. This image was probably an

Symbols of
Trinity

attempt to dispel the notion that the Son sacrificed Himself to placate the Father and to emphasise that the work of redemption involved all Three Persons of the Godhead e.g. Childrey, Berks. (brass); Doddiscombleigh, Devon (glass); Kinlet, Salop. (alabaster); Lichfield St. John Baptist, Staffs. (boss); Orford, Suff. (font); Selworthy, Som. (boss); Snape, Suff. (font); Tideswell, Derbys. (brass); Willoughby-on-the-Wolds, Notts. (tomb); York Holy Trinity Goodramgate (glass).

Other symbols include three interlaced circles, three interlaced triangles ('Solomon's seal'), a triangle superimposed on a circle, the trefoil and the popular heraldic device illustrated which occurs e.g. Cowfield, Sussex (brass); Cirencester, Glos. (glass).

The individual persons were distinguished generally as follows:
Father – old man with beard, sometimes with papal tiara and orb: Malvern, Worcs. (glass).
Son – with a cruciform nimbus and indications of His Passion.
Spirit – as a Dove, usually haloed.

Angelic trumpeter

TRUMPETS AND HERALDS
May symbolise preachers who trumpet the call to action, proclaim the King and transmit His laws and commandments. The angel of the Annunciation sometimes carries a herald's baton. Trumpets, particularly in the hands of angels, may refer to the end of the world (II Cor. 15.52; Rev. 8.2).

TUTIVILLIUS
A demon active during the occasions of liturgical prayer. He collected in a sack the words omitted or syncoped by careless clerks as well as writing down the idle words of those who joked or gossipped in church e.g. Charlton Mackrell, Som. (bench-end); Colton, Norf. (mural); Drayton, Berks. (alabaster); Ely cathedral; Enville, Staffs.; Gayton, Northants. (misericords); Little Melton, Norf.; (murals); Oxford New College, (misericord); Peakirk, Northants.; Seething, Norf. (murals).

A warning inscription on the wall-plate at Churchtown, Lancs. advises the congregation of this demon's activities. In mystery plays and

145

Tympanum

other literary sources he is associated with
'blowing his own trumpet' e.g. Campsall, Yorks.;
Canterbury cathedral crypt, (capital);
Dorchester, Oxon. (corbel). 'Tittyvally', a
favourite expression of Thomas More's wife and
others, known to Shakespeare, is probably a
corruption of Tutivillius or Tittivillius.

TYMPANUM
The space enclosed between the horizontal
lintel and the enclosing arch in Romanesque
and Gothic doorways, often filled with ornament
or sculpture of a symbolic nature e.g. Aston
Eyre, Salop.; Barfreston, Kent; Elkstone, Glos.

TYPES
Old Testament figures or events which
foreshadow the Christian dispensation. Christ
himself referred to the serpent in the wilderness
and the story of Jonah as figures of His own
crucifixion and resurrection while St. Paul
found a type of baptism in the Israelites'
crossing of the Red Sea. Typology was much
employed in Old Testament exegesis and accounts
for much of mediaeval imagery e.g. Isaac bearing
the faggots is a type of Christ bearing the Cross
(Worcester cathedral misericord) as his sacrifice
prefigures Christ's (Malmesbury, Wilts. porch;
Malvern, Worcs. glass).
   Samson breaking the lion's jaws is a type of
the Harrowing of Hell e.g. Bristol cathedral
(misericord); Highworth, Wilts. (tympanum);
Paignton, Devon (chantry carving); Stretton
Sugwas, Herefs. (tympanum). His carrying away
the gates of Gaza typifies the Resurrection e.g.
Malmesbury, Wilts. (door); Norwich cathedral
nave (boss); Paignton, Devon (chantry carving);
Ripon cathedral (misericord). Gideon's fleece is
a type of the Virgin Birth e.g. Fairford, Glos.
(glass) and the Spies from Canaan of the
promise of Heaven e.g. Ripon, Yorks. (misericord).

Samson: harrowing of
hell

UNCTION   see also *Oil; Sacrament.*
Ceremonial anointing with oil derived from
Old Testament usage where prophets, priests
and kings were anointed as a mark of their
vocation and of Divine favour. The Church uses
oil in some sacraments and in certain
blessings and consecrations. The word is most

often used of the anointing of the sick,
misleadingly called extreme unction. It symbolises
consecration and commission and Durandus
connects extreme unction with the 'rubbing down'
of athletes to prepare them for the contest.

UNICORN   see *Fabulous Beasts*.

VAULTING
Durandus sees roof-vaulting as symbolising
preachers and this would explain the didactic
subject-matter of roof-bosses (q.v.) though they
would seem to presuppose an abnormal acuity
of vision for their full effect.

Roof vaulting

VEIL
Veiling, whether of a person (nun, bride) or of a
thing (altar, chalice), generally represents some
kind of dedication or consecration. Lenten veils
(q.v.) are an exception. Veils also indicate
mystery and screen holy things and places from
profane view. Mediaeval churches had a veil or
screen separating nave from chancel and, for a
time, one separating altar or sanctuary from
quire. The symbolism is derived from the Jewish
temple and from the Epistle to the Hebrews.
These veils represented tradition, reverence and
the veiled nature of God.

VERGE   see also *Wands of Office*.
Gives name to Verger who originally carried a
mace or verge before an ecclesiastical dignitary
or procession. Such rods or staffs originally
symbolised power or fertility — 'rod' is a
frequent image in the Old Testament, especially
associated with Moses, Aaron, Jesse. A verge may
symbolise Christ or the Virgin Mary. Gabriel,
particularly in Annunciation scenes, may hold a
herald's baton. Churchwardens in Anglican church
have staffs, one tipped with a mitre (for the
parish priest's warden), the other with a crown
(for the people's warden).

Verge

VERNICLE   see *Veronica*.

VERONICA
There is a legend that, as Christ was carrying his
Cross to Calvary, a woman pityingly wiped His
face with a linen cloth which then received the

147

Vernicle

imprint of Christ's face. This is called the vernicle and is included among the Passion emblems e.g. Altarnum, Cornw. (bench-end); Bacton, Herefs. (paten); Beeston Regis, Norf. (paten); Hessett, Suff. (burse); Leominster, Herefs. (paten); Salisbury St. Edmund (paten); Winchester cathedral choir (boss); Yarnton, Oxon. (reredos). The woman, given the name Veronica, is commemorated in the sixth of the Stations of the Cross (q.v.).

VESICA PISCIS

The pointed oval or almond-shaped mandorla which often surrounds representations of Christ in Glory (see Majestas), probably derived from Ezekiel 1.26; Revelation 4.2). It is a symbol of heavenly glory and when executed in mediaeval stained glass becomes a glowing nebulous splendour. 'Vesica piscis' means 'a fish bladder', which is somewhat of this shape. This mandorla is mostly given to God, occasionally to the glorification of Virgin Mary (Assumption) and, even more rarely, to represent the glory of the souls of the blessed.

VESSELS, SACRED

Chalice: cup in which wine is consecrated, symbol of blood, suffering, communion. Attribute of St. John Evangelist.

Paten: small circular dish or plate on which bread is consecrated.

Both chalice and paten are said to symbolise the tomb in which Christ rested. Representations mark the tomb of a priest and they were often buried with him.

Chalice

Ciborium: cup with close fitting lid to contain Hosts (consecrated wafers). See Pyx.

These altar vessels were normally made of precious metals (gold or silver) and few survive from the middle ages e.g. Bacton, Herefs.; Beswick, Yorks.; Hamstall Ridware, Staffs.; Leominster, Herefs. There is a chalice at Goathland, Yorks. and patens at Beeston Regis, Norf.; Donnington, Sussex; Salisbury St. Edmund, Wilts.; Wyke, Hants.

VESTMENTS

Eucharistic vestments are frequently depicted as are other kinds of ecclesiastical dress as well as

Paten

Vestments

the formal dress of lawyers, physicians, master-masons etc.

The eucharistic vestments (derived from the 'best clothes' of the Romans) were given symbolic significance.

amice (A): linen head covering, helmet of salvation.

alb: loose full-length long-sleeved garment of white linen, purity.

cincture: woollen girdle with tassels, self-restraint.

maniple (C): ornamental band on left arm (originally kerchief), trials and good works.

stole (B): Ornamented scarf-like garment worn over shoulders, cross and grace.

chasuble (D): uppermost mass vestment of priest, charity.

dalmatic: similar tabard-like garment of deacon, joy.

tunicle: sub-deacon's vestment almost indistinguishable from above, joy.

All but the first three are made from rich materials, elaborately decorated (often with symbolic motifs) and change colour with the season (see Liturgical colours).

cope: a cloak-like garment, richly embroidered used in choir and for processions.

surplice: shorter version of alb, sometimes with sleeves, choir habit.

mitre: head-dress worn by bishops and some abbots, symbol of authority and of the 'cloven tongues' of the apostolic commission (Acts 2.3). Other head-wear: skull-cap, cowl, academic cap and tiara (q.v.).

Crosier: ornamented crook, symbol of pastoral responsibility since it was used to goad, guide and rescue by shepherds.

e.g. brasses at Castle Ashby, Northants.; Dorchester, Oxon. (abbot); Higham Ferrers, Northants. (mass vestments); Oxford New College (pontificials).

VEXILLUM
Banner or pennant inscribed with cross, symbol of victory (over death, corruption and evil). Usual attribute of resurrected Christ and of Agnus Dei (q.v.).

VIRGIN MARY
Blessed Virgin, St. Mary the Virgin, Our Lady etc. Became a growing object of Christian

Virgin Mary

devotion from the earliest centuries, the most frequently portrayed of the saints and the one with the greatest number of dedications. In spite of the Reformers' iconoclastic fury against this devotion many representations survive e.g. Axminster, Devon (tomb); Beaumaris, Anglesey (brass); Bigby, Lincs. (sculpture); Cowlam, Yorks. (font); Fovant, Wilts. (brass); Fownhope, Herefs. (tympanum); Inglesham, Wilts. (Saxon cross); Morley, Derbys. (brass); Nunburnholme, Yorks. (Saxon cross); Sculthorpe, Norf. (font); Shelford, Notts. (Saxon cross); Warkworth, Northants.; Willoughby-on-the-Wolds, Notts. (tombs).

The most popular representation was of the Virgin and Child e.g. Inglesham, Wilts.; Sennen, Cornw. which is also depicted on glass at e.g. Eaton Bishop, Herefs.; Fladbury, Worcs.; Gresford, Denbighs.; Ludlow St. Lawrence, Salop.; South Cerney, Glos.; and on murals at Bramley, Hants.; Great Canfield, Hadleigh, Essex; Hampstead Norris, Berks.; Mentmore, Bucks.; Stone, Kent.

In C15, the Pieta (Mary holding the dead body of her Son) became popular e.g. Battlefield, Salop. (sculpture); Breadsall, Derbys. (alabaster); East Harling, Norf.; Leverington, Cambs.; Long Melford, Suff. (glass); Orford, Suff. (font).

Depictions of her 'mysteries' in the Rosary (q.v.) are extremely common e.g. Ashton, Devon (screen); Beverley minster, Yorks. (alabaster); Brook, Kent (mural); Chilton Canteloe, Som. (mural); Cobham, Surrey, (brass); Cold Overton, Leics. (mural); East Hagbourne, Berks. (glass); Fovant, Wilts. (brass); Gresford, Denbighs. (glass); Long Melford, Suff. (alabaster); Newcastle St. Nicholas, Northd. (font-cover); Plymtree, Devon, (screen); Purton, Wilts. (mural); Ripon, Yorks. (alabaster); Sutton Bingham, Som. (mural); Warkworth, Northants. (bench-end); York St. Helen, (glass).

The life of the Virgin is depicted at Croughton, Northants. (mural), she helps to carry Christ's cross (Blunham, Beds.) and stands with John at the foot of the Rood (q.v.). Her burial occurs at Stoke d'Abernon, Surrey and Chalgrove, Oxon. and she intercedes for humanity on Doomsday at Patcham, Sussex.

The symbolical significance of the Virgin lies in the total co-operation between a human being and God in the working out of the Divine Purpose.

The Virgin's attributes are blue robe, veil, lily and her emblems (see Arma Virginis) include a lily, a pierced heart, a crowned M or MR (e.g. Mendlesham, Suff.) a closed gate (Coventry Holy Trinity; Norwich cathedral), and a garden enclosed.

VIRTUES AND VICES see also *Corporal Works of Mercy; Sins.*

Fall of pride

Virtues were classified under seven headings within two divisions:

Cardinal: Fortitude, Justice, Prudence, Temperance – open to all people of good-will.
Theological: Faith, Hope, Charity – specifically Christian.

Durandus says that the 'virtues are depicted under the form of women because they soothe and nourish' e.g. Salisbury cathedral chapter house (door); Southrop, Glos.; Stanton Fitzwarren, Wilts. (fonts).

The seven deadly sins were not only symbolised and personified but antidotes against them were provided: the Lord's Prayer, meditation on the Instruments of the Passion (q.v.) with accompanying prayers, exemplars and intercessors – Sussanna against lechery, King Robert against pride, Clare against gluttony, James against wrath and cruelty, Anthony and Denis against envy.

Symbolic edification was provided via bosses and grotesques, bench-ends and misericords in which e.g. a torch may stand for lechery and a bowl of water for the opposing virtue of temperance. Conflicts between knights or between men and beasts often represent the 'Psychomachia', the soul's warfare between virtue and vice.

Lechery

The virtues of Mercy, Truth, Righteousness and Peace were called 'the daughters of God' (Camb. King's College chapel; Tattershall, Lincs. (glass). King's College glass also portrays the allegorical 'Holy Hunt' (which may also be symbolised in angel choir, Lincoln cathedral) where Gabriel drives these same virtues as hounds to direct Christ (cf. unicorn) into lap of

151

Virtue: St. Edward

Vice: sloth

Virgin Mary. For other virtues and vices see e.g. Barwell, Sussex; Blythburgh, Suff.; Hoxne, Suff.; Raunds, Northants.; Ruislip, Middlesex; Thornham, Norf.; Trotton, Sussex.

Both virtues and vices are seminal, with ramifications and inter-relations. The theological virtues (I Cor. 13) are nourished by prayer, sacraments and sacramentals and each of the cardinal virtues embraces a spectrum of ideals and action and they all spring from some aspect of love. Conversely, vices centre on the Satanic sin of Pride, replacing God by self, objective virtue by subjective value. Envy includes blasphemy and swearing is often a concomitant of Avarice. Lust means inordinate (i.e. irrational) desire for anything but is often typified by lechery. Gluttony includes drunkenness and is associated with Lust (luxuria). Sloth includes neglect of religious duties and spiritual apathy. Avarice leads to fraud which is opposed to Justice; Anger may arise from gambling and suicide may have elements of sloth and despair which is opposed to hope etc.

Symbols of vices include:

Pride: lion, Lucifer, peacock.

Covetousness: urchon (hedgehog), griffin, ape tied to clog, spider sucking fly. 'Ale-wife' seems to symbolise fraud.

Wrath: wolf, hedgehog, toad (also symbolises heresy which is product of pride and wrath).

Envy: hound.

Sloth: Ass, bear (also symbolises gluttony because he gorges himself on the fruit of others' labour (bees)).

Gluttony: bear, hound chasing hare, fox carrying off goose, 'miredromble' (a fabulous bittern-like bird as large as a swan and possessed of two stomachs.).

Lust (Luxuria): centaur, mermaid, swine.

Symbols can combine reference and refer either to association or to opposite. An image of a vice was also meant to conjure up the opposed virtue, an opposition which was sometimes made explicit e.g. Fishlake, Yorks. (door). A symbol might be multi-faceted e.g. Judas' suicide (wrath, despair, treachery as opposed to charity, hope, faith). The same symbol may serve more than one purpose e.g. David's conflict with Goliath may signify conflict between good and evil or between work and sloth (though mediaevals did not regard work, per se, as a virtue).

VISITATION
Mary's visit to Elizabeth (Lk. i.39ff.) also called 'Salutation', associated with 'Magnificat' (q.v.) e.g. Paignton, Devon (chantry).

VOTIVE
Something given or consecrated in fulfilment of a vow; simply an offering, perhaps with a special intention. Votive candle: before statue, shrine or relics — 'The candle does not dispense with prayer but continues it. It does not dispense with sacrifice but symbolises it'. Votive offerings represent thanks for favours received and include inscriptions, models, entire chapels and scratches on the wall (see Graffiti).

The Visitation

VOW
A solemn promise, taken seriously in Middle Ages and often fulfilled at very great cost including pilgrimages, religious foundations e.g. Battle Abbey, Sussex; Vowchurch, Herefs.

VOWESS   see *Religious Orders.*

WALL PAINTINGS
Their appreciation requires more effort than other mediaeval survivals since time, decay, deliberate destruction and insensitive restoration have done their work but, with a little imagination and time, some idea of the originals may be gathered e.g. Barfreston, Kent; Baunton, Glos.; Chaldon, Surrey; Easby, Yorks.; East Wellow, Hants.; Fairstead, Fingringhoe, Essex; Flamstead, Herts.; Fritton, Suff.; Glatton, Hunts., Great Canfield, Essex; Hessett, Suff.; Hauxton, Cambs.; Idsworth, Hants.; Kempley, Glos.; North Leigh, North Stoke, Oxon.; Oaksey, Wilts.; Pickering, Yorks.; Wenhaston, Suff.

Wall painting of
St. Christopher

No imagination can restore those that have completely vanished e.g. the Corporal Works of Mercy which once graced the exterior wall of High Wycombe, Bucks., but knowledge of symbolism, particularly that associated wtih saint's days and other festivals and with the

153

'Verdant with
various flowers'

theological and moral teaching of the mediaeval
age will help. The aim of the overall decorative
scheme, including the mural painting, is well
expressed by the monk Theophilus, writing
c.1100 A.D.:

'Animated, dear son, by these covenants with
the virtues, thou hast confidently approached
the House of God, hast decorated with the
utmost beauty ceilings or walls with various
work, and showing forth with different colours
a likeness of the Paradise of God, glowing with
various flowers, verdant with herbs and leaves
and cherishing the lives of saints with crowns
of various merit. Thou hast, after a fashion,
shown to beholders everything in creation
praising God, its Creator, and hast caused them
to proclaim Him 'wonderful in all His works'.
Nor is the eye of man able to decide on which
work it may first fix its glance: if it regards the
walls, there is the appearance of Paradise; if it
marks the abundance of light from the windows,
it admires the inestimable beauty of the glass
and the variety of the most costly work. But if
perchance a faithful mind should behold a
representation of our Lord's Passion graphically
represented, it is penetrated with compunction;
if it beholds how many sufferings the saints have
supported in their bodies, and how many rewards
of eternal life they have received, it quickly
induces the observance of a better life; if it
regards how much rejoicing is in Heaven and
how much suffering in the flames of Hell, it is
animated by hope for its good actions and is
struck with fear by the consideration of its sins.'

WAND   see also *Verge*.
The sceptre or wand is a symbol of authority or
of commission. The Blessed Virgin Mary has
often the attribute of a wand, particularly in
representations of her glorification. It is usually
tipped with a triple bud, recalling the fleur-de-
lys (see Lily), symbolising the Trinity with
whose redemptive work she is associated and her
possession of the three theological virtues (see
Virtues and Vices). Her peculiar sceptre has
other symbolic associations: instrument of God,
Tree of Jesse, Incarnation. e.g. Cowlam, Yorks.
(font); Willoughby-on-the-Wolds, Notts. (tomb).

Wand

Washing feet

Holy Water

WASHING FEET   see also *Maundy Thursday*.
Mary washing Christ's feet was a symbol of
penitent love e.g. Leonard Stanley, Glos.
(capital); West Horsley, Surrey (glass).

WATER   see also *Font; Piscina; Stoup; Well*.
'Water is an emblem of the Holy Spirit.'
(Durandus). Its obvious associations are with the
source and maintenance of life and with
cleansing. Its life-symbolism is central to font and
baptism but there is a rarer and vivid image at
Kilpeck, Herefs. where the bowl of the holy water
stoup images the belly of a pregnant woman. Holy
water was so much used in the Middle Ages that the
minor clerical job of aquifer often supported
university students. It was frequently used in the
blessing of houses but especially at the beginning
of every mass in a ceremony called the Asperges
when the congregation were sprinkled with Holy
Water during the singing of Psalm 1. with the
antiphon 'Thou shalt purge me with hyssop and
I shall be cleansed'.
    Blessing oneself with Holy water (see Stoup)
is a reminder of baptism, of the need for a pure
heart with which to approach God and perhaps
a reminder that human life and time flow away.

WEAPONS   see also *Conflict; Tools*.
Some are included under Instruments of Passion
(q.v.). Generally, they appear either as an
attribute of a saint, indicating the mode of his
martyrdom, or they symbolise vices e.g. the
falchion is a symbol of wrath, the spear of envy.
They may also appear in representations of the
conflict between virtue and vice.

WEATHER VANE
The cock is usually a symbol of St. Peter in
reference to his denial of Christ (Matthew
26.69–75) but the cock on weather-vanes
signifies Christian watchfulness and the necessity
of preaching Christ at all season and in all
directions (e.g. Alford, Surrey):
    'For the cock, ever watchful even in the depth
of the night, giveth notice how the hours pass,
wakeneth the sleepers, predicteth the approach
of day, but first exciteth himself to crow by
beating his sides with his wings. There is a

Weather vane

Weather vane

mystery conveyed in each of these particulars. The night is this world, the sleepers are the children of this world asleep in their sins. The cock is the preacher who preacheth boldly and exciteth the sleepers to cast away the works of darkness, exclaiming "Awake thou that sleepest and Christ shall give thee light" . . . and as the weathercock faceth the wind, they turn themselves boldly to meet the rebellious. . .' (Durandus).

The vane is not always in the form of a cock e.g. Buxted, Sussex (trumpet); Etchingham, Sussex (heraldic device); Piddinghoe, Sussex (dolphin); Torver, Lancs. (fish); Walsingham shrine, Norf. (angel).

WEEPERS

Diminutive figures surrounding tomb (not to be confused with ranks of children) who represent mourners or intercessors for the soul of departed. They may be bedesmen (particularly in relation to founders or benefactors of chantries or hospitals), usually old men and women who receive alms from the foundation on condition that they pray for the repose of their benefactor e.g. Bakewell, Derbys.; Reepham, Norf.

WELLS AND SPRINGS   see also *Wounds*.

Wells and springs were often sacred sites before the arrival of the Christian mission but many of them have associations with missionaries or have been otherwise Christianised. Wells near a church are often under the same patronage. There are holy wells at Avon Dassett, Warks.; Shadwell (St. Chad's well), Yorks.; St. Neot, Cornw.; Walsingham, Norf. There are wells in or near the church at e.g. Bawburgh, Norf.; Bodmin, Cornw.; Marden, Herefs.; Needingworth, Hunts. The holy wells at Giggleswick and Middleham, Yorks. seem to have engendered the patron saint Alkelda, said to have been martyred by the Danes (depicted in glass at both places), but 'Halig-keld' could simply mean 'Holy Well'. Well-dressing persists in Derbyshire, usually on Ascension Day e.g. Tideswell, Tissington, Youlgreave, and also at Bisley, Glos.

WHEEL

A very common symbol apart from its occurrence

Weeper

Wheel

as an attribute of St. Catherine. It may be derived from Ezekiel (1.15–21) and symbolise the 'dynamism' of God. Wheels can be an attribute of the seraphim (see Angelic orders) e.g. Cirencester, Glos. (cope); Treyford, Sussex (glass).

Heaven was conceived as a musical wheel and the mediaevals also had a wheel of lust or sensuality (often with a butterfly resting on it), wheels of life e.g. Kempley, Glos.; Leominster, Herefs., wheels enclosing the corporal works of mercy or the seven deadly sins and rolling the involved to heaven or hell.

Wheels can also be an attribute of patriarchs, prophets or those apostles who were not evangelists and in this connection seem to symbolise imperfect revelation. The significance of the wheels at Legerwood, Berks.; Stoke Orchard, Glos.; Thornham Parva, Suff. is obscure.

WILD MAN (WOODWOSE)   see also *Jack o' the Green.*
Usually depicted with shaggy hair over all his body and seems to symbolise unregenerate man e.g. Happisburgh, Norf. (font); Tattershall, Lincs. (brass). He is sometimes in conflict with an archer e.g. West Rounton, Yorks. (font) or with a lion e.g. Acle, Ludham, Norf. (fonts). Other appearances at e.g. Coventry Holy Trinity, Warks. (misericord); Haverhill, Suff. (tower); Lincoln, Norwich cathedrals (misericords); Tewkesbury St. Edmund's chapel (boss).

Some representations of unusually hirsute men may refer to the legend of the Hairy Anchorite e.g. Idsworth, Hants. (mural)?

Windmill

WINDMILL
Variety of symbolic meanings: turning without grinding represents sloth or the passage of time; or it may signify the heavenly bread bought by men ground by the stones of derision which are powered by the winds of fury. It is also an attribute of St. Victor. e.g. Baunton, Glos. (mural); Bishops Lydeard, Som. (bench-end); Fairford, Glos. (glass); Gawsworth, Ches. (mural); North Cadbury, Som. (bench-end); St. Mary-in-Marsh, Kent (chalice); Thornham, Norf. (bench-end); Tor Bryan, Devon (screen) and bench ends elsewhere in county.

157

Window

WINDOWS

From the invention of Gothic architecture windows were associated with light-symbolism and light itself was seen as a most appropriate symbol of God. Lancet windows arranged in triplets almost certainly refer to the Holy Trinity (the legend of St. Barbara makes three windows a symbol of Christian belief). Two associated windows over the west door probably signifies the Two Natures of Christ. Trefoliated tracery would seem to have a Trinitarian reference.

Wheel windows have been interpreted as emblematic of St. Catherine but this is an unlikely interpretation (see Wheel). They are probably symbols of the universal, of the totality of creation or of the circle of eternity.

'The glass windows in church are Holy Scriptures which expel the wind and the rain, i.e. all things hurtful, but transmit the light of the True Sun, i.e. God, into the hearts of the faithful. Windows are wider within than without because the mystical sense of Scripture is ampler than the literal meaning and precedes it. Also, the senses of the body are signified by the windows because the senses should be shut to the vanities of the world and open to receive spiritual gifts with all freedom.' (Durandus).

WINGED CREATURES   see also *Angels; Dragons; Monsters.*

Wings symbolise speed and have a supernatural connotation (see Ezekial 1.5–14). Man's head with wings e.g. Ely cathedral Lady chapel; winged monsters e.g. Beverley St. Mary, Yorks.; cherubim with monsters e.g. Chivelstone, Devon (screen). Usually a winged face represents a cherub. The emblems of the evangelists (q.v.) are all winged: man, lion, ox and eagle.

Winged creature

WITCHCRAFT

Regarded as a sin of the most profound malignity since it included both blasphemy and malice and thus offended deliberately against the highest commandments: love of God and love of neighbour. It seems to have been represented on murals at Crostwick, Norf.; Wiston, Suff.

WITS (SENSES), FIVE

His five wits represented man's contact with the

sensible world and they were intended to be the ordered servants of reason and conscience. Wheels of the senses used to exist in churches, there is a representation of this motif on Anglo-Saxon silver and Five-Wits is a personified in morality plays e.g. Everyman. No wheels of the senses survive in any church but there is one at Longthorpe Tower, near Peterborough, Hunts.

WORDS, IDLE　　　see also *Jangling; Tutivillius*.
Profane swearing by God or his attributes (Zounds — By God's Wounds; Bloody — By our Lady?) was much condemned as sacrilege in the Middle Ages and there were iconographic warnings against the practice e.g. Broughton, Bucks. (mural). There were similar warnings against what may seem the lesser sin of chattering e.g. Colton, Norf. (mural); Ely cathedral, Cambs.; Enville, Staffs.; Gayton, Northants. (misericords); Little Melton, Norf.; Peakirk, Northants.; Seething, Norf. (murals).

Wounds

WOUNDS　　　see also *Five Wounds*.
From the time of St. Augustine it had been believed that wounds received in God's service on earth would be marks of glory in heaven, hence the saints are often depicted with instruments of their martyrdom or the bodily injuries. This belief was pre-eminently true of Christ's wounds which remained after His resurrection. Devotion to them was possibly stimulated by St. Francis and his stigmata (q.v.). In devotional literature and sermons they were sometimes called 'Wells' of Wisdom, Mercy, Eternal Life, Grace, Good Comfort e.g. Bowness-on-Windermere, Cumb.; Froyle, Hants.; Marston Bigot, Som. (glass); North Cadbury, Som. (bench-end); Sidmouth, Devon (glass).

WRESTLERS　　　see also *Conflict; Games. . .*
May merely depict sport but this is probably a superficial explanation in view of St. Paul's remarks (Eph. 6.12) and the Old Testament story of a revelation of God after Jacob had wrestled with an angel (Genesis 32.24f.) e.g. Ely cathedral, Cambs.; Halsall, Lancs. (misericords); Lechlade, Glos.; Lincoln cathedral (bosses).

Cross Saltire

X   see also *Chi-rho*.
Cross saltire, the symbol of St. Andrew who was
supposed to have been crucified on a cross of
this shape.

YGGDRASIL

The sacred tree of Norse mythology e.g. Heysham,
Lancs. (hog-back q.v.). It was probably the yew
which is often found in church yards and some
examples may be older than the church itself e.g.
Aldworth, Berks.; Darley Dale, Derbys.;
Etchingham, Sussex; Overton, Hants.; Ulcombe,
Kent.

Yews were formally sacred and symbolised
life and immortality, hence the yew hedges in
churchyards e.g. Hound, Hants.; Painswick, Glos.
Because of their symbolism they were used for
Easter decorations and their twigs and branches
were sometimes utilised on Palm Sunday (q.v.)
instead of the foreign palm.

YULE

A Germanic pagan feast, lasting twelve days,
connected with the winter solstice which was
absorbed into the Christian festival of the
Unconquerable Sun. The Yule-log seems to be
a combination of fire- and tree-worship.

ZODIAC

Individual signs (Leo, Sagittarius) may represent
Christ e.g. Kencott, Salford, Oxon., Stoke-sub-
Hamdon, Som. but generally the zodiac seems to
be a symbol of time as opposed to eternity. It
could also signify order; the stars in their courses
which manifest the power and wisdom of their
Creator. The Zodiac occurs on the chancel arch
at Copford, Essex and may denote the transition
from earthly existence through the heavens to
Heaven itself as it occupies the division between
the nave (earth) and the chancel (heaven).
Together with the Labours of the Months (q.v.)
the Zodiac provides a terrestrial calendar e.g.
Barfreston, Kent (door); Bredon, Worcs.
(sanctuary steps); Brookland, Kent (font); Egleton,
Rutl. (door); Hastings All Saints, Sussex (boss);
Hook Norton, Oxon. (font); Iffley, Oxon. (font);
Oxford Merton College (gateway boss); Stratford-
sub-castle, Wilts. (clock-face); West Rounton,
Yorks. (font); York St. Lawrence (door).

Zodiac

LAVS DEO

FURTHER READING

For general architectural and artistic matters the appropriate
county volume of N. Pevsner's monumental 'Buildings of
England'. For general and specific matters of building and
sculpture the works of F. Bond (now out of print) and in a
single volume J. C. Cox — Parish Churches of England (London
1941). The works of M. D. Anderson are fascinating,
particularly perhaps 'Imagery of British Churches' (London
1955). For roof-bosses the authority is C. J. P. Cave: Roof-
bosses in Mediaeval Churches (London 1948), for wall-painting
— E. W. Tristram: separate volumes on C12, C13 and C14
(1944, 1950, 1955). For stained glass you might consult
J. Baker: English Stained Glass (1961), for brasses: J. Franklyn
'Brasses' (1964) — particularly good on inscriptions. The same
author has a useful book on heraldry 'Shield and Crest' (1960).
For background in preaching: G. R. Owst and for an available
bestiary T. M. White: The Book of Beasts (1956). For general
architectural symbolism. E. Male: The Gothic Image (1961)
and for symbolism in more detail: G. Ferguson: Signs and
Symbols in Christian Art.

INDEX OF PLACES

Places are attributed to old counties in accordance with Bartholomew's 'Gazetteer of the British Isles' (1966). This is not only due to antipathy towards bureaucrats but also to facilitate the use of supplementary material e.g. Pevsner.

A page reference may contain more than one allusion to the place mentioned.